Melville

He who has never failed somewhere,
that man cannot be great.
Failure is the true test of greatness.

MELVILLE.

Pacific Ocean
Sep. 2d 1860

My Dear Bessie: I thought I would send you a letter, that you could read yourself— at least a part of it. But here and there I purpose to write in the usual manner, as I find the printing style comes rather awkwardly in a rolling ship. Mamma will read those parts to you. We have seen a good many sea-birds. Many have follot -wed the ship day after day. I used to feed them with crumbs. But now it has got to be warm weather, the birds have left us. They we about as big as chickens.— They were, all over speckled— and they would

JEAN-JACQUES MAYOUX

Translated by John Ashbery

Melville

Evergreen Profile Book 9

GROVE PRESS, INC.   EVERGREEN BOOKS, LTD.
NEW YORK   LONDON

ENGLISH DISCOGRAPHICAL DETAILS REVISED BY PETER GAMMOND.
FIRST PUBLISHED IN THIS EDITION 1960. ALL RIGHTS RESERVED.
Library of Congress Catalog Card Number: 59-7541
Evergreen Profile Books are published
in the United States by Barney Rosset at Grove Press Inc.
64 University Place   New York 3, N.Y.
in Great Britain by Evergreen Books, Ltd.
17 Sackville Street   London, W. 1
Distributed in Canada by McClelland & Stewart Ltd., 25 Hollinger Rd., Toronto 16
First published in France by Editions du Seuil, Paris
MANUFACTURED BY MOUTON & CO., IN THE NETHERLANDS

Melville
by Jean-Jacques Mayoux

Contents

DESCRIPTION

Age 37 Years

Stature 5 Feet 8¾ Inches Eng.ᵈ

Forehead Medium

Eyes Blue

Nose Straight

Mouth Medium

Chin Round

Hair Dark Brown

Complexion Fair

Face Oval

————— >:< —————

Herman Melville

Chronology

1819   Birth of Herman Melville, August 1, in New York.
        Birth of Walt Whitman.
        Publication of Washington Irving's *Sketch Book*.
1826   Melville has scarlet fever. His eyesight will remain permanently weak
        as a result.
1830   Allan Melville liquidates his business in New York and moves to
        Albany.
        Herman leaves school and goes to work in a bank.
1837   Gansevoort Melville goes bankrupt.
        Herman teaches school.
        Hawthorne's *Twice-Told Tales*.
        Emerson's *The American Scholar*.
1839   Melville embarks as cabin boy on the *Saint Lawrence*, bound for
        Liverpool.
        Poe's *Tales of the Grotesque*.
1840   (December) Melville embarks on the whaling ship *Acushnet*.
        Cooper's *The Pathfinder*.
        Dana's *Two Years Before the Mast*.
1841   At sea.
        Emerson's *Essays, First Series*.
        Cooper's *The Deerslayer*.
        Poe's *Murders in the Rue Morgue*.
        Inauguration of Brook Farm, the transcendentalists's utopian com-
        munity.
1842   (July) Herman Melville deserts the ship at Nukuheva.
        (July-August). He remains at Typee.
        (September-October). He visits Tahiti.

Mutiny and hangings aboard the brig *Somers*.
Longfellow's *Ballads and Other Poems*.

1843 (August) Herman Melville takes service on the frigate *United States*.
Birth of Henry James.

1844 (October) Herman Melville disembarks at Boston.
Gansevoort Melville campaigns for James Knox Polk, the Democratic candidate for the presidency.

1845 Melville writes *Typee*.
Polk is elected. Gansevoort Melville is given a post in London, where he grants the rights to *Typee* to the publisher John Murray.

1846 Publication of *Typee* in England and the United States.
Melville writes *Omoo*.
Hawthorne's *Mosses from an Old Manse*. Emerson's *Poems*.
Poe's *The Philosophy of Composition*.
Mexican War.
Birth of William F. Cody (Buffalo Bill).

1847 Publication of *Omoo*.
(August) Melville marries Elizabeth Shaw, of Boston.
They settle in New York.
Longfellow's *Evangeline*.
The Mormons settle in Utah.
Birth of Edison.

1848 Melville writes *Mardi*.
Gold is discovered in California.

1849 Melville writes *Redburn* and *White Jacket*.
Publication of *Mardi*, then of *Redburn*.
(October) Melville leaves for England.
Thoreau's *A Week on the Concord and Merrimack Rivers*.
The gold rush.

1850 Back in New York, Melville writes *Moby Dick*.
(August) Melville meets Hawthorne.
(September) Melville buys a farm near Pittsfield, Massachusetts.
Publication of *White Jacket*.
Hawthorne's *The Scarlet Letter*. Emerson's *Representative Men*.

1851 Publication of *Moby Dick*.
Hawthorne's *The House of the Seven Gables*.

1852 Publication of *Pierre*.
Hawthorne's *The Blithedale Romance*. Harriet Beecher Stowe's *Uncle Tom's Cabin*.

1853 Publication of *Bartleby the Scrivener* in *Putnam's Monthly Magazine*.

1854 Melville writes *Israel Potter*, which begins appearing in *Putnam's Monthly Magazine* in July.
Publication of *The Encantadas* in *Putnam's Monthly Magazine*.
Thoreau's *Walden*.

1855 Publication of *Israel Potter*.
Publication of *Benito Cereno* (in *Putnam's Monthly Magazine*).
Whitman's *Leaves of Grass*.

1856 (October) Melville sails for Europe. Meeting with Hawthorne.
Melville writes *The Confidence Man*.
Publication of *Piazza Tales*.

1857 Trip through the Holy Land. Return to America.
Publication of *The Confidence Man*.

1858 Melville makes two lecture tours. He writes poems.

1859 Third and last lecture tour.

1860   Cruise on board the *Meteor*.
1861   Melville tries to obtain a diplomatic post.
       Secession of the southern states. Beginning of the Civil War.
1862   Melville sells his farm.
1863   New York.
1866   Melville becomes customs inspector.
       Publication of *Battle Pieces* (poems).
1870   Melville begins writing *Clarel*, a long poem.
1876   Publication of *Clarel*.
       Whitman's *Leaves of Grass* (Centenary Edition).
       Mark Twain's *The Adventures of Tom Sawyer*. Henry James's
       Roderick Hudson.
1885   Melville resigns his post.
1888   Publication (in a limited edition) of *John Marr and Other Sailors*
       (poems).
       Melville begins writing *Billy Budd*.
1891   Melville finishes *Billy Budd*.
       Death of Melville on September 28.

Pastry cutter made by the whale hunters
from a whale's tooth.

The Gentleman's Son

Herman Melville (in those days the family spelled their name Melvill) was born·in New York, August 1, 1819. On both sides of the family, his ancestry was a distinguished one.

Major Thomas Melville of Boston had been among those who, one memorable day in 1773, had dispatched a cargo of English tea into the brackish waters of Boston harbor, thus inaugurating the battle for American independence. When the war·came, General Peter Gansevoort played a glorious role in it. These men were Melville's two grandfathers. General Gansevoort, whom James Fenimore Cooper was to recall as one of the close friends of his youth, is "Old Pierre," the prodigious ancestor whose image obsesses young Pierre in Melville's novel of that title, in which he also invented an opulent Gansevoort childhood, spent on vast ancestral estates. It is the mothers who create family mythologies; thus Herman's mythology was based on the power and prestige of the great Dutch settlers (or poltroons) of the Hudson Valley, a region we tend more to associate with the carefree, tattered spirit of Rip Van Winkle.

Major Thomas Melville does not appear in the work of his grandson. Nonetheless he was an almost legendary figure, whom Daniel Webster was to evoke in 1832 as "a personification of the

11

Major Thomas Melville, one of the grandfathers.

His son Allan Melville, Herman's father.

spirit of 1776, one of the first to venture in the cause of liberty," though neither his work nor his reputation were enough to secure him in 1829 against the "spoils system," fiercely promoted by the new and vigorously democratic president, Andrew Jackson.

Major Melville was in that year relieved of his post in the Boston customhouse. Time in the United States had already begun to pass quickly and cruelly. "The people," in whose name Jackson was acting, had already begun jostling the old aristocracy and attacking the new forces of plutocracy.

The Major had had eleven children, of whom Allan, Herman's father, was the fourth. We know him through the portion of his correspondence which has been preserved, which contains a wealth of noble sentiments rather pompously displayed: against slavery, for instance, which he held was a disgrace to the nation. He was the owner of an import firm in New York. The former New Amsterdam, only yesterday a modest colonial port, had begun mushrooming rapidly, with a hundred thousand inhabitants in 1810 and over two hundred thousand in 1820. One might be tempted to think that this giddy rise in population had brought about a corresponding facility of operations in the business world, but

13

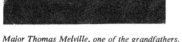

The fabulous ancestor: General Peter Gansevoort, Melville's other grandfather.

nothing was farther from the truth. If ever free enterprise and fierce, brutal competition flourished under ideal conditions, it was in America during the first half of the nineteenth century, especially in New York. Allan Melville could invoke in his letters as much as he liked his noble ancestors at Flodden Field and other battles: business remained the same. More and more he was being forced to ask for loans, in terms fraught with high-flown justifications, either from the Major in Boston or from his brother-in-law, Peter Gansevoort.

Meanwhile Maria Melville, his wife, kept up appearances as though nothing were the matter, and frequently gave children's parties. If Allan professed that rather vague kind of Christianity, popular among the upper classes of the youthful republic, known as Unitarianism, Mary remained faithful to the Calvinist faith of her fathers but not the somber, austere, menacing faith described in Hawthorne's tales of the puritans. It had become rather a matter of easy compromises, of principles given lip service. Predestination, the impossibility of salvation if one is not among the saved, had become a bogey-man to frighten the children with.

Yet such was the spiritual heritage of the incredibly naive young Herman Melville.

In general these untroubled early generations were oriented toward the "pursuit of happiness" as the Declaration of Independence had proposed. Nonetheless they could not afford to neglect business. Allan's was liquidated in September, 1830, and the family retreated to Albany, where its head died raving mad, January 28, 1832, leaving enormous debts behind him.

What effect did the catastrophe have on young Herman? His father's letters sometimes round out his childish silhouette with a sudden firmness that takes one by surprise: "He is very backward in speech & somewhat slow in comprehension, but you will find him as far as he understands men & things both solid & profound, & of a docile & amiable disposition...."

He is seven years old. Three years later, at school: "Herman is making more progress than formerly, & without being a bright Scholar, he maintains a respectable standing, & would proceed further if he could be induced to study more – being a most amiable & innocent child, I cannot find it in my heart to coerce him, especially as he seems to have chosen Commerce as a favorite pursuit."

Is this delay "in speech" already the outward sign of certain inhibitions like that mental laziness and torpor, which we shall

14

observe a little later on? This commercial vocation comes as a surprise to us: perhaps its only significance is that of piety toward the image of the father which will last throughout his life, and which, as a child, inspired him to imitation.

Was he loved by his mother? In *Pierre* he will be the adored and adoring only son. But this may be a compensation for reality. Before this, in a curious passage in *Moby Dick* he describes the child Ishmael punished by a hard-hearted stepmother, exiled from the immense summer sun in the false night of his bed, and there, between sleeping and waking, invaded by a characteristic vision of guilt: "At last I must have fallen into a troubled nightmare of a doze; and slowly waking from it – half steeped in dreams – I opened my eyes, and the before sunlit room was now wrapped in outer darkness. Instantly I felt a shock running through all my frame; nothing was to be seen, and nothing was to be heard; but a supernatural hand seemed placed in mine. My arm hung over the counterpane, and the nameless, unimaginable, silent form or phantoms, to which the hand belonged, seemed closely seated by my bedside. For what seemed ages piled on ages, I lay there, frozen with the most awful fears, not daring to drag away my hand; yet ever thinking that if I could but stir it one single inch, the horrid spell would be broken. I knew not how this consciousness at last glided away from me...."

De Quincey recalls similar haunting impressions of his childhood, and we know that Melville was strongly influenced by the writings of the "opium eater." But it is hard to believe that this was a factual account of experienced terrors which pursued him throughout life. Something is in contact with him, he who is in contact with nothing. Something knows him, he who as yet knows nothing. The young sailor perched in the crow's nest is plunged by the rhythms of the waves into a kind of hypnosis: in this reverie "I...expected to hear myself called to, out of the clear blue air, or from the depths of the deep blue sea." Joseph K, that is to say Kafka, heard himself similarly called to in the empty cathedral.

Herman was not yet thirteen when he and his elder brother, Gansevoort, were removed from school (that "Academy" of Albany where the decorum of his social class still surrounded him) in order to expiate the unknown sins of his father. While Gansevoort Melville (the family name of one clan had become the given name of the other) who was only seventeen, tried bravely to manage unaided a fur and felt factory, Herman became an ordinary clerk in his uncle Peter Gansevoort's bank. With the coming and to the degree that it is American, it is local. Washington Irving founded the Knickerbocker School, attempting to create around retrograde New York the sleepy charm of the English provinces. Fenimore Cooper evoked a more ancient past, one which the new civilization had almost completely stamped out, and lamented the passing of the noble Indian and the wilderness. Gansevoort Melville read *The Prairie*, and Herman will long remember the pleasure he savored in reading *The Red Rover*. Later he will write of Cooper: "His works are among the earliest I remember as in my boyhood producing a vivid and awakening power upon my mind."

But we see from the first essay he has published in a local newspaper that, already inquisitive, he was on familiar terms with "Old Burton's *Anatomy of Melancholy*." On the other hand, he confides in *Moby Dick* that when he saw his first albatross, regal, dazzling, "a prodigy of plumage," he did not know what bird it was. "I had not then read the rhyme [of Coleridge]."

After shipping out for the first time, in the autumn of 1840, at a time when he was feeling spiritually as well as physically at sea, he will discover Richard Henry Dana's *Two Years before the Mast*, one of the first books in which the spirit of America revealed itself; in which anxiety creates a need for physical, manual action, and finds an equilibrium in vigor and derring-do. Melville, writing to Dana, attested his feeling of a "sort of Siamese link of affectionate sympathy" with the hero and the evocator of this rugged saga of the sea.

At the beginning of June, 1839, after eight years of insecurity and instability, Melville found the solution that he will later playfully compare to suicide. At twenty he had already tried a number of jobs, experienced uncertainty, unemployment, the vain hunt for work. And so he took a job as cabin boy on the *Saint Lawrence*, a merchant ship sailing for Liverpool. On June 5th, he was in the open sea.

Redburn, written some ten years later, will be the autobiography of this first adventure. Melville always held the book in contempt, since, writing down to the public, he had put into it neither literary refinements nor psychological subtleties. This is true. But his precise, concrete descriptions are a revelation. On the very first page, in the first paragraph, the theme of humiliating poverty is sounded. The harshness of the world and the times have had their effect, says the author, on the aching heart of young Redburn: "I had learned to think much and bitterly before my time; all my young mounting dreams of glory had left me; and at that early age, I of summer he was left all alone at his job, his mother and the other children having fled to the country to escape a plague of Asiatic cholera. Uncle Peter married, and his brother's family became more and more of a burden to him. Herman left the bank. We find him again managing another uncle's farm, then teaching in a school with no budget, intermittently pursuing vague studies. These diverse occupations were interrupted by wanderings to find new ones. The two clans grew poorer. The young men took to the sea without much hope of success. Some cousins on both sides of the family became midshipmen, and in 1835 Thomas Melville and Leonard Gansevoort embarked on whaling vessels. In 1837 it was Gansevoort Melville's turn to go deeply bankrupt. In spite of everything, Herman continued to lead on the surface the life of a member in good standing of that society which still remained colonial, that is, doubly provincial. In Albany he joins the "Young Men's Society and the Philologos Debating Society."

What is the cultural atmosphere of his world? In general it knew nothing of the romantic movement and combined a belated classicism with precocious Victorianism. It is not very national,

The old Gansevoort home, near New York.

was as unambitious as a man of sixty.... There is no misanthrope like a boy disappointed, and such was I, with the warm soul of me flogged out by adversity.... Talk not of the bitterness of middle-age and after life; a boy can feel all that, and much more.... And never again can such blights be made good; they strike in too deep, and leave such a scar that the air of Paradise might not erase it. And it is a hard and cruel thing thus in early youth to taste beforehand the pangs which should be reserved for the stout time of manhood."

We must avoid oversimplifying. The Melville who embarked on the *Saint Lawrence* did not choose the sea out of simple despair. Childhood dreams, echoes of his father's voyages, memories of the books of Captain Marryat, magic and exoticism – all these, Melville rightly points out, were mingled with the necessity to earn a living. The naive romanticism he attributes to himself was no doubt very real, with its vision of how he would look returning from distant lands, superbly clothed, bronzed by the sun, catching every eye, ready to tell his adventures to eager listeners. But it is also obvious that these dreams of prestige, involving both the cabin boy and the writer, are the sign of a soul extremely sensitive to the opinions of others, horribly conscious of itself as a spectacle, one moment glorious, grotesque the next; always making the first move, donning the grotesque mask "of its own accord," making use of that more or less subtle self-mockery which is a sense of humor.

At the very beginning, the leitmotif of clothes projects us into the middle of the Melvillian universe. Wellingborough-Herman and his family are so impoverished that when it comes time to fit him out for going to sea, nothing can be found but a hunting jacket belonging to the eldest brother. "The scent and savor of poverty was upon me." He leaves Albany for New York with barely a dollar to pay his fare on the river-boat, which owing to a change in price, now costs two. He feels the "cold suspicious glances" of the well-fed bourgeois passengers fixed on him, and feels that despair mingled with defiance "which only a pauper knows." After first trying to hide the patch in his pants, he shows it off, defying the world's opinion.

Once aboard the *Saint Lawrence*, he reveals another, complementary aspect of his character; after the revel among the bourgeois, we meet the snob who refuses to be confused with the common riffraff. Confronted with a captain who is presumably a man of breeding, but who is actually (and here Melville sounds his favorite theme of the reality behind appearances) as base of heart as he is of ancestry, the hero tries to strut, to show himself as coming from a good family: "My great-uncle, the senator..." For a moment the captain seems an image of the father; the cabin boy tries to meet his "free, frank look": the disillusion is a cruel one, the solitude seems more painful, and Redburn all the more grotesque for having lost several precious dollars at this game played against a shrewd, unscrupulous cynic.

Wellingborough's ridiculous efforts to establish social relations with the captain are equaled only by the care he takes to keep the crew at a distance. Like Dickens wanting to remain at any price the "little gentleman" in the blacking-factory, so Wellingborough-Herman carries with him his past as a delicate, well brought up young man, a nonsmoker and member of temperance societies. "I strove to talk in Addisonian English." And as a matter of fact one never hears him speak without thinking that he had just taken an elocution lesson, and the too-cultivated voice will be a trade-mark of the Melvillian hero from book to book, in *Moby Dick* and even in *Pierre*.

His misadventures are many and burlesque. Everyone tries to humiliate the young man who has lost his social standing, from the captain down to the last member of the crew: the first task assigned to him is to clean the pigpen. His clothes are jeered at as the visible symbol of his inability to adapt himself: the ridiculous high-heeled boots which almost carry him overboard several times, and the famous jacket worn as a symbol. Shrunken by rain and seaspray, it becomes more and more skimpy and painful to wear, like the conventions of social caste for a young man flung brutally into the midst of life. It is a cruel apprenticeship that Melville forces us to witness: an initiation not only to pain and danger, but above all, to the terrible world of the forecastle, of humanity as it really is—coarse, brutal, sinister, and stupid; initiation to Evil and those mysteries represented by the ascendancy, authority, and energy of evil embodied in the sailor Jackson. One thinks: how Melville must have suffered!

In Liverpool, still wearing the tight-fitting jacket, this young foreigner, so grotesque-looking that people instinctively turn aside to let him pass, cannot help remembering the figure his father cut there in former days, "in a blue coat, buff vest, and Hessian boots." What a contrast between that fashion plate and the orphan whom people shoo away whenever he ventures near the fashionable districts formerly frequented by his father. Without resentment "I

The years of apprenticeship.

always thought him a marvelous being, infinitely purer and greater than I was."

But something is burgeoning within him, secretly and in spite of himself. The father still remains the venerated guardian of values. But the values he protects have begun to decompose by themselves, lighting him up with the livid glow of their dissolution. One of the most curious symbols of the book is the *Guide to Liverpool*. Wellingborough-Herman arrives with his father's guidebook in hand: "My own father had used this very guide book, and thereby it had been thoroughly tested, and its fidelity proved beyond a peradventure."

To retrace his father's footsteps, to find his old home — these are the first objectives of this "filial pilgrimage."

It is impossible to tell with certitude which parts of *Redburn* belong to the experience of 1839 and which parts are the result of the moral drawn from it in 1849; which characteristics belong to Melville the writer and which to the cabin boy Redburn. But the excursion in the English countryside, with its rebuffs, its manifestations of man's hatred for man, and finally the scene where scorn and contempt are assuaged in a home where he meets three charming young girls, remains meaningful, whether invented or not. The episode is significant because of its stilted quality and its unconvincing female characters, defined by an accumulation of clichés. The narrator forces himself to describe his infatuation and regret for this female trio which he never manages really to envisage. It is hard to marry three women at once, but this does not prevent Redburn from declaring, more in earnest than in jest, that he will remain a bachelor in memory of these three charmers. One wonders whether, consciously or unconsciously, this episode was not inserted here to balance that which immediately follows, curiously coupled with it: the scene in which Redburn meets Harry Bolton. "He was one of those small, but perfectly formed beings, with curling hair, and silken muscles, who seems to have been born in cocoons. His complexion was of a mantling brunette, feminine as a girl; his feet were small; his hands were white; and his eyes were large, black, and womanly; and poetry aside, his voice was as the sound of a harp."

This collection of female characteristics is not the exclusive property of Harry. Among the immigrants on the return voyage, a little Italian boy named Carlo will also display "a naked leg as beautiful to behold as any lady's arm; so soft and rounded." But the close friendship with Harry Bolton is the first of a series which one notes throughout the life and work of Melville. In almost all of the novels there is a handsome sailor: Toby in *Typee*, Jack Chase in *White Jacket*, the mysterious Bulkington in *Moby Dick* and finally Billy Budd in the novella of that name.

Harry is a gambler and good-for-nothing, lazy, a pathological

liar, whose charm is described rather than projected by Melville. He is a young aristocrat, or at any rate sufficiently well brought up to give himself airs, and to consummate his own ruin with an insouciance mingled with somber paroxysms, as befits a romantic rake. Wellingborough is unable to resist his influence, and together they run off to London on a wild escapade that is described in a strange, dreamlike passage: through these glorious reveries one remarks that the lost child, reassured at having found a friend, is re-creating a world in which to take refuge.

But this sentiment of human brotherhood has also penetrated to him through the sight of suffering, misery, and misfortune. What an unforgettable and darkly romantic vision is that of the woman starving to death with her children clinging to her tatters in a dungeon in the waterfront section of Liverpool; soon we see the unforgettable picture of their death agony replaced by a pile of quicklime. Human pity swells his heart. This prospect on humanity, unusual in Melville's work at this early stage, is matched by a frank, vigorous style which we shall find again in the dramatic evocation of the epidemic which during the voyage home decimates the emigrants, too ignorant to meet it face to face and struggle against it.

His voyage over, Herman rejoined his family during the first

The slums of Liverpool
(engraving by Gustave Doré)

days of October, 1839. He found the same poverty, its hues a little deeper this time, and the same dread of tomorrow, now even more of an everyday phenomenon. He arrived at the very moment that the sale of Maria's furniture was announced. She immediately sent him to his uncle Peter, to beg for alms: they had become their only source of livelihood, and her letters express both her distress and her bitterness at finding herself in need, her humiliation at having always to call for help: "It cannot be possible that I am to be left by my two brothers to struggle with absolute want, or be compelled to write painful truth-speaking letters, descriptions of our situation, to ward off by a reluctant remittance, our present wants...." Remittances so insufficient that once she finished paying the most pressing debts, there was nothing left over.

Immediately on his return Herman took a post as schoolmaster, but he seemed to have great difficulties in getting paid. In June, 1840 he was once again a prey to uncertainty: the impossible atmosphere of the family home would be enough to explain this. Persuaded by his friend Eli Fly, he went off on one of those escapades which punctuate his existence as a young man eternally out of work, unfitted for life – and this at the very moment when he was naively paying court to a young girl. In life as in *Redburn*, the meeting with Harry Bolton follows that of the three young girls.

On December 26, 1840, Melville was at New Bedford; the 31st, he took the vital step in his life – he signed his name in the register of a three-masted whaling ship, the *Acushnet*, captained by Valentine Pease. "The crew," he writes to his brother some months later, "is much superior in morale and early advantages to the ordinary run of whaling crews."

On January 3, 1841, the *Acushnet*, which will become the *Pequod* in *Moby Dick*, sets sail from New Bedford. Thus began the rude adventure, the interminable descent toward the southern whaling banks across a waste of empty sea. Six months later, on June 23, 1842, the whaler cast anchor in Nukuheva Bay. On July 9, Melville deserted, accompanied by the eternal "buddy," or perhaps accompanying him. It is the adventure he recounts in *Typee*.

Toby Green is a type similar to Harry Bolton, a romantic comrade. "No one ever saw Toby laugh." On the one hand, the sailor who prefers the outcast solitude to the vulgarity of the crew, finds in him affinities of class as well as of temperament. "He was one of that class of rovers you sometimes meet at sea, who never reveal their origin, never allude to home, and go rambling

26

over the world as if pursued by some mysterious fate they cannot possibly elude." On the other hand, he has the same physical charms as Harry – at any rate they are evoked in the same language. He is "singularly small and slightly made, with great flexibility of limb. His naturally dark complexion had been deepened by exposure to the tropical sun, and a mass of jetty locks clustered around his temples, and threw darker shade into his black eyes." He is strange, capricious, melancholy, passionate: he exerts a strange kind of domination over the common horde.

In the country of the Typees.

On August 9th, exactly one month later, Herman Melville, seaman, was inscribed in the register of the crew of the *Lucy Ann* and set sail from Nukuheva. The ship's log bears no reference to a romantic deliverance of the seaman in question in the bay of Typee. We shall never know what really happened to Melville during the brief space of a month between one ship and the other, which leaves him about three weeks among the "cannibals." When *Typee* appeared and the critics, not wanting to be duped, proclaimed it sheer invention, R. T. Greene, who happened to

exist and decided to put his old adventure to profit, wrote in turn *The Story of Toby* to back up his former companion. But since they spent only a few days together on the island before being separated, Toby actually cleared up nothing, and confirms, briefly, only this: that they had spent some time together with the dreaded Typees who allowed Toby to depart, while Melville, hurt and unable to walk, remained with them. The rest is, broadly speaking, literature. We shall speak of it again.

Omoo takes up the story of Herman at the moment when, escaped from Typee, he embarks, still more or less lame, on a whaling vessel from Sydney, the *Lucy Ann*. Together with *Redburn*, the book that is the least reworked of any of Melville's, it is that which is closest to the period of the events he narrates with so much freshness. He portrays himself as a carefree child, a young, robust vagabond, lusting for the freedom of the vast highroads of earth and sea, vigorously despising all rules and restraints.

Judging from the proportions of the mutiny which broke out when the *Lucy Ann*, after having put its captain ashore at Tahiti, was proceeding onward under the command of the first mate, there seems no doubt that it actually was a ship in a bad way, badly run by a weak and sickly captain. Melville had been aboard a month when, with numerous companions, he refused to obey any longer. The rhythm of the changes in his life that summer of 1842 is almost dizzying.

The mutinous sailors were transferred to land where a picturesque and primitive jail awaited them, run by an easygoing native jailer. It was simple for Melville to escape, towards the middle of October, in the company of his new comrade, Long Ghost, who for once seems not to have been an Adonis, but the most genial of specters. In spite of Melville, Long Ghost (an ex-ship's doctor), appears as one of those drifters who from generation to generation rot slowly away on the shores of some Pacific island. And yet this is not completely true. Greedy, lecherous, possessed of a powerful thirst for alcohol, lazy to the point of ostentation, Long Ghost seems the stronger of the two, a *sanguine* personality. One has the impression that Melville followed timidly in his footsteps.

What a paradise of rustic games, exotic fruit, and also of girls! Long Ghost seems to have paid court to them with a vigor that Melville reports discreetly. Of the latter's own activities we know nothing. In Tahiti, he had at least been interested by the handsome Kooloo: "As for Kooloo, after sponging me well, he one

The cannibal Eden.

morning played the part of retrograde lover; informing me that
his affections had undergone a change...."

He depicts the young Tahitian girls as above all terrorized by
the missionaries and watched over by the neophytes, but nothing
seems to indicate that he felt greatly disturbed by them. On the
contrary, one day he is "startled by a sunny apparition. It was
that of a beautiful young Englishwoman." She gallops swiftly
away on her horse. He discovers that she is the wife of a sugar
planter, Mr. Bell, whom he visits. But she has left that very morning
for Papeete. Conclusion: "To my dying day, I shall never forget
Mrs. Bell." Two years later, when he is at work on *Redburn*, he
will vow himself to eternal bachelorhood (in reality he was already
married), in memory of the three English girls. He loves ideal and
idealized figures. Lieutenant Henry Wise, travelling through
Tahitian waters in 1848, inquired about the characters in *Omoo*
and noted: "Charming Mrs. Bell took to hard drink – before
Mr. Melville's rencontre." Of course the character of the swoon-

31

ing lover is amusing to the public, and Melville loves to don a false nose and put on an act. But the gratuitous, repeated choice of this theme suggests a less conscious intention, and causes one to think that Melville was glad to give a wrong impression of his own peculiarly frigid (rather than perverted) nature. This would be enough to explain the slightly sickening quality of everything approaching eroticism in his work.

After several weeks, Melville had exhausted the pleasures of idleness, had had enough of the carefree vagabond life, and, in my opinion, was frankly bored. In short, on November 7, 1842, approximately a month after his escape from the Calabouza Beretani in Papeete, Melville bids farewell to Long Ghost and embarks on the good ship *Charles Henry*, where he was perhaps a harpooner, if indeed he ever was one in his life. He leaves the ship at Lahaina in the Hawaiian Islands, but on August 17, he embarks once again on the frigate *United States*. His instability is more marked than ever at a time when he is about to be yoked to the hard, cruel, almost ferocious discipline of an American battleship of those days. We are not surprised at the vehemence with which, in *White Jacket*, he denounces corporal punishment, the colt and the cat-o'-nine-tails whose blows humiliate the soul even more than they hurt the body. *White Jacket* is an indictment of cruel and unjust authority and its hateful violation of all that is human, and at the same time it poses the question of real authority which would probably be that of the father. But it is the protective personification of an ideal and glorious brotherhood whom he finds on board ship in the person of Jack Chase. This first captain of the top, intuitive, magnanimous, an ardent reader of Camoens, is doubtless with Hawthorne one of the two men in his life for whom Melville experienced the most exalted and passionate feelings, since fifty years later he was to dedicate *Billy Budd* to him, in strangely fervent terms.

Jack Chase is the angelic figure, the mediator whom Melville must have in order not to feel alone in the world of men, and whom he seems to have found nowhere else endowed with so much natural nobility. Jack radiates generosity and, in the real sense of the word, self-integrity, which is just what Melville lacks. The latter, confronted with his hero, is once more a stranger made ridiculous by his clothes. Redburn's hunting jacket is replaced by a white jacket Melville made for himself, which absorbs water and holds it like a blotter and which, in addition to its discomfort, fills the other sailors with aversion and a superstitious dread. In the story, the narrator falls into the water at almost the very moment the ship arrives in the harbor and almost drowns, weighted down and paralyzed by the white jacket. It has been discovered that this superb passage was based on a seaman's yarn Melville had read. In reality, he no doubt contented himself with throwing the accursed garment overboard, as he writes in a letter to Dana of May 1, 1850. "It was a veritable garment – which I suppose is now somewhere at the bottom of Charles River. I was a great fool, or I should have brought such a remarkable fabric (as it really was, to behold) home with me." Symbolically, he had, in order to save himself, ripped from his body the white jacket of self-affirmation, egotism, pride in humiliation, and a penchant for misfortune. But in reality Melville had an inexhaustible stock of white jackets that were not lying at the bottom of the Charles River.

One day aboard the frigate, the narrator is condemned to be whipped for having been absent from a post to which he was not assigned. The monstrous shadow of injustice has fallen upon him, as it will upon Billy Budd. Billy Budd's fist will fly out automatically, in a sort of daze of horror. The narrator in the white jacket has time to reflect and decides to throw himself overboard, dragging the captain along to his destruction: Jack's intercession saves him. If the scene is invented, or inspired by some other, it is none the less *authentic*, in the sense that Melville discovered himself in it and thus revealed himself to us. The intensity of the tone is a guarantee of this: "My blood seemed clotting in my veins; I felt icy cold at the tips of my fingers, and a dimness was before my eyes. But through that dimness the boatswain's mate, scourge in hand, loomed like a giant, and Captain Claret and the blue sea seen through the opening at the gangway, showed with an awful vividness."

What Melville threw into the Charles River along with the white jacket was not selfishness, it was his humble lot as a sailor. But no doubt he realized nothing of this. When he arrived in New York he was so disheveled and dirty that his brother made him tidy himself up before he met their mother. Once cleaned up, he was going to be able to play the fabulous role of the voyager full of memories for his mother and sisters and the little world of Lansingburgh.

He began to tell his story, and, according to his first biographer, one of his listeners suggested that he write them down just as he told them. It would have been surprising if the idea had not already come to him.

The Cannibals

"Until I was twenty-five," wrote Melville to Hawthorne in 1851, "I had no development at all." That is, until he returned from his voyages, until he stopped living (in the sense of the word which limits life to activity in the external world) and began to think about himself. Everything happened as though, in comparison with the violent shocks of his childhood, his adolescence and young manhood had been, in the guise of brutal activity, like that of war, nothing but escape, flight, numbing of conscience. That sensitive, imaginative young Calvinist conscience will return gradually from whence it was banished by those first shocks.

Nonetheless in 1845 there is no question of his returning to his inner resources. The man in the hunting coat, in the white jacket, the man in the ridiculous clothes, seated in the midst of an admiring public, is about to clothe himself with charm and good humor. He is at once at home in his role of the story-teller: "Yes, reader, as I live...." His neurotic need for support and sympathy causes him to assume as a matter of course the role of the ancient mariner, to seek out the comfortable nearness of the dazzled public. It is not merely the truth of actual facts which is involved in the episodes where he appears as a historian, it is above all a matter of romantic authenticity, or the writer's loyalty to himself, the degree of honesty in the description of the emotions he attributes to himself and which he intends to make the reader share with him.

Typee begins with the arrival in Nukuheva bay of the whaling vessel from which the narrator and his friend are to make their escape. It is rather difficult for us to imagine how two men who are free to remain on board, who are fleeing neither from danger nor unbearable living conditions, who have merely "had enough" of the terrible monotony of the days on shipboard, can desert in

The Queen of Nukuheva.

the full realization of what their situation on the island is to be that Melville attributes to them. They will not be able to stay at Nukuheva, he tells us, where they would be either captured by the crew or ransomed to them by the natives. Their only recourse is to scramble up from the harbor into the abrupt jungle about which they know nothing save that on the other side two valleys converge, one of which is inhabited by Happars, rather decent folk, and the other by monstrous cannibals, the Typees.

Under these circumstances their flight amounts to the inexplicable choice of martyrdom. Always in the back of their thoughts, in a tumult of vague fears, is the precise dread of being eaten alive; the first time they see the footprints of the savages (they were quite aware that they were bound to run across savages in the jungle) they feel the same terror that Robinson Crusoe felt – except that for the latter the footprints meant the sudden overwhelming break with solitude.

Meanwhile they have one harrassing certainty: that of physical pain. And the dilemma remains intact: *Typee or Happar?* As a matter of fact, the footprints turn out to be those of Typees.

One can't help feeling that the young teller of tales has endowed his own tale with a suspense that is still slightly naive. Cannibals have always played a large role in children's books, and we must not lose sight of this tantalizing fact. In bringing his sailor boys to Nukuheva, Melville reveals their anticipations: "Lovely houris – cannibal banquets," and one can only say that the Typees fulfill the program and that there is no point in twisting an adventure story to extract profound meanings from it. We must content ourselves with remarking that while the public especially noticed the naked houris, their role is insignificant, while the obsession with cannibals dominates the book heavily. The importance of this misunderstanding is all the greater if it is unintentional, if the author deviated from his plan as though compelled to.

Typee or Happar? The principal problem is not that of knowing which they will meet, but *how they will recognize them*, how they will be able to tell the good Happars from the bad Typees. It is the problem of the ambiguity of appearances, broadened into a fundamental ambiguity, for ultimately it is no clearer how a Happar, recognized as a Happar, can be recognized as good, than how a Typee can be recognized as bad. We are in the presence of the first formulation of the great enigma which is to consume Melville – the eternal ambivalence of the universe, of its good or evil intentions toward us. Terror is always ready and waiting in our

hearts, and it is profound.

D. H. Lawrence read *Typee* much too quickly, and was thus able to construct a marvelous theory of it based on psychoanalysis*: may-be Melville experienced in the cannibal garden of Eden a purely sensual animal happiness against which his white-man's conscience finally rebelled; and, of course, the "symptom" appeared: his leg began to swell up and refused to support him any longer. But Melville's leg had begun to swell in the bush, almost at the beginning of his flight, and before he had had any contact with Eden. The savages find a lame man whom they care for and cure – only temporarily, it is true.

The cannibals, seen objectively, are charming. Melville is able to write about these inhabitants of Eden in the style of Bougainville, if not that of Diderot. He sees clearly that original sin did not happen here, that the soul and body form a single whole. This leads him to the idea of the flawless beauty and grace of these naked men and women.

---

* *Studies in Classic American Literature*, D. H. Lawrence.

Melville insisted on the documentary aspect of what he wrote, even though he often refreshed and, if need be, supplanted his memory through his reading. He thus builds up a generous description of the life and customs of this people, in line with liberal European thought from Montaigne to Diderot, in the spirit of the *Aufklarung*. The Typees are good savages, children without conscious morals, but nonetheless provided with an innate morality, a mutual respect for persons and goods – that is, the few objects which, excluding the earth and its fruits, make up their private property. There is no money on Typee, but there is abundance and fraternal love. As for the cannibalism, it is all nothing but the inventions of missionaries crying wolf, slandering the civilizations they want to destroy. If, all the same, there is an occasional instance of cannibalism, this is not the result of perversity or refined gastronomic tastes, but a kind of sacred vengeance wreaked against the enemies one has conquered and killed,

The friendly savages of Tahiti

and which is no worse than any other kind of vengeance. These are all rational, optimistic considerations, worthy of the eighteenth-century philosophers. They are hard to reconcile with the dramatic narrative in which they are set down and whose dominating note is one of suffering.

The actual experience of sensual ecstasy does not appear in the book, and what sensuality there is is given a curiously passive twist: as the narrator lets himself be anointed and perfumed by a group of beautiful girls, so he abandons himself to the tender attentions of Fayaway. But one wonders if it is merely an accident that the pleasure most often described as experienced by the couple is that of boating. Doubtless, Victorian America was squeamish to a fault, and Melville was obliged to suppress a scene from the second edition in which a native queen shows her behind. But in any case this was a burlesque episode, and it is hard to deduce from this a personal censorship so effective that it left the book, in spite of its subject matter, completely devoid of erotic suggestion.

Such is not the case with the reality of suffering. One might simplify grossly and say that that story proceeds from suffering to further suffering through the illusion of a happiness beyond time: "I can scarcely understand how it was that, in the midst of so many consolatory circumstances, my mind should still have been consumed by the most dismal forebodings, and have remained a prey to the profoundest melancholy."

When he wishes to appear carefree, he gives just the opposite impression: "I gave myself up to the passing hour, and if ever disagreeable thoughts arose in my mind, I drove them away."

True, it is often difficult to decide whether this suffering is part of the remembered adventure, whether it has been inserted by the novelist for effect, or whether it does not rather indicate, in its deliberate warping of memories, a profound and revealing psychological need.

In the perspective of the story, the joking which makes cannibalism seem like a cliché of macabre humor ("For what do you suppose the devils have been feeding us up in this kind of style?" asks Toby who feels it would be best to starve oneself) is followed by a fearful silence or sleep, which is in turn succeeded by the dramatic, or melodramatic, tumult of the discovery of the remains of a human banquet of slain enemies. The horror awakes terror; we are far from rational or quasi-ethnological considerations now. These are no longer the same cannibals; they are no longer *com-*

"For what do you suppose the devils have been feeding us up?"

mensurable; they have become a strange monstrosity, an object of horror and wild fright. The temptation to rejoin Toby at all costs, the day he hears rumors of a ship in the harbor, becomes irresistible for the hero – but it runs up against the inflexible authority of Mehevi, whose menace has become insistent. "It was at this moment, when fifty savage countenances were glaring upon me, that I first truly experienced I was indeed a captive in the valley."

Such terror was surely experienced; none the less surely it has been arranged for the purposes of the novel, and, if we are to believe the internal evidence and the credibility of the deeds and happenings reported, it seems scarcely likely that the departure from the valley took the form of a desperate flight, of the final fight with knives and boat-hooks and of the curious triumph over the powerless gesticulations of the savages, which seems to belong to some half-literary, half-dreamlike world. Finally, behind the faking in *Typee*, whose exact extent we cannot determine, one feels that Melville is trying not so much to pull the wool over the reader's eyes as to recapture, were it merely in inventions and story-telling which seem to contradict his actual experiences, something deep within him which reveals something of his true nature.

The gentle Fayaway can do nothing against it, nor the handsome Marnoo, nor the good fortune to have come in real life upon the eternal mirage of the fortunate isles. The cannibals are more *essential* to Melville. Collectively they constitute a kind of dark, gaping mouth ready to swallow him up. The cannibals are his first Leviathan and *Typee* is ultimately a symbolic allegory.

But, snug in the intellectual comfort of its salons, its newspapers and magazines, the American public of 1846, still half-colonial, uncertain just what literature was and what it was searching for, chose to acclaim in this first work of a unknown storyteller, with minor reserves – little gestures of frightened prudery which seemed like encouragements – a delectable mixture of humor, adventure, exoticism, and sensual dallying. The sea-dog author was sought after and feted. People saw him, touched him, and all was well. But also they wanted to know if the adventure was true, if things had really happened that way, if there had been a Fayaway. The national vulgarity, born long before Hollywood and its movie stars, reveled in the event, while at the same time the ministers fretted and issued condemnations, and families looked askance at their daughters for reading the book.

In London, where Gansevoort Melville had just obtained a minor diplomatic post, the book, published by John Murray, had

42

exactly the same ambiguous success. In London as in New York the second edition was expurgated, especially the passages against missionaries. The revulsion, still imperceptible, had already begun.

Melville did not long remain idle. An interval of only a few hours separates the story of *Typee* from that of *Omoo*; and he paused scarcely longer before beginning the new work – actually the day he first began writing with so much apparent facility, it is as if a long brainfever had begun. At first it is noticeable only as a pleasant warmth.

Following so closely on its heels, *Omoo* in comparison with *Typee* gives an immediate feeling of stylistic assurance, acceleration, and activity. The words are charged with feeling; the right adjectives come up, the whole is strongly imaged: "... The grim, black spars and waspish hull of a small man-of-war craft crept into view.... ...Before long, what seemed a live ember rested for a moment on the rim of the ocean, and at last the blood-red sun stood full and round in the level East, and the long sea-day began."

Melville has been practicing, and in a few months has learned to see and to speak. But even more certainly the success of his first book has relaxed and reassured him for the moment. He is authorized by himself and his public to assume this nonchalance, this ease. The book is a long, pleasant stroll. The crumbling, worm-eaten aspect of things and (up to a certain point) of people aboard the *Julia*, everything including disease and death are treated here lightly and casually. Themes are proposed, certain symbols seem to lend themselves to an allegorical visionary treatment, but Melville remains in the realm of the tangible; he keeps the themes in reserve, and leaves the symbols their mysterious limpidity. Yet it is unmistakably Melville's world, the world he carries about with him, still with the air of not being completely aware of it. One night in the stiflingly close quarters of the forecastle, the cold, clammy hand of a dying man touches that of the narrator. One day Bembo the Maori, the native harpooner, leaps onto a whale in his fury at having missed it with the harpoon. Then after a fight in which the crew sides against him, Bembo becomes the enemy, "that man, or devil," writes Melville, a figure of avenging hatred who finally tries to run the ship aground on the reefs. Bembo is a forerunner of the harpooners in *Moby Dick* and even has some of Ahab's intensity. But the existing order of things is not yet endangered by this individual disorder.

When the ship docks at Tahiti, the tensions on board the *Julia* are no longer anything but a comic theme. This joyfully egoistic book is the least egotistic that Melville wrote, that in which he most accepts himself as he was, and not as he was trying to be. It is the book in which there is the most equilibrium between the ego and the outside world. It is surprising that a mind still so immature could bring so much human lucidity to its examination of the problem of the already irreparable genocide perpetrated by the missionaries on the soul of the Tahitians. Fraternity among men and among races, sympathy for the oppressed and denunciation of the oppressors will remain one of Melville's central themes. But nowhere will it burst forth as spontaneously as in *Omoo*, nowhere is the fundamental principle on which Melville bases this absolute brotherhood more clearly related to the character of the author himself as he appears in the book. This time the *Aufklarung* is total and unopposed. Melville is not content merely to praise the inborn grace and virtue of the Tahitians, nor to evoke a past full of constructive activity, of devotion to the useful and creative arts, which are not lacking in a kind of grandeur. The great canoes, the beautiful native huts, the subtle *tapas*, everything whose manufacture was interrupted when the people stopped hoping, enters into this noble elegy. Nor is he content merely to relate the misfortunes and degrading oppression resulting from the decrees of the missionaries, who have reduced the natives to a physical and moral inertia painful to behold. He shows the dignity of their intellectual resistance to the preaching and dogma which are crushing them: "We want no other salvation than to live in this world. Where are there any saved through your speech?"

Melville defined his book for Murray as "a comic sojourn in Tahiti." The goodhearted simplicity and half-cynical frankness with which he describes this vagabond existence, characterized by a horror of all work; the drollery of the portraits, everything invites the reader to appreciate *Omoo* as a typical comic novel. Melville will never go farther than this toward attempting to depict reality. A better book than *Typee*, *Omoo* is probably less typical of its author.

In any case Melville, whose brother Gansevoort has just died apparently insane in London, seems himself to be in amazing physical and mental good health. He is still immersed in the joy of his success, his sudden fame. He insists, without too much sincerity, on the authenticity of *Typee*. Toby's reappearance in life is providential: it seems to prove the truth of everything, and Melville constantly invokes Toby's existence as a kind of argument. *Omoo* is published and produces the same chorus of enthusiasts, the same indignant protests. It is fame's double aspect. In the midst of his fame, Melville marries. A curious marriage! No name appears oftener in the handout-begging correspondence of Herman's father, Allan Melville, than that of Judge Lemuel Shaw. He has remained a family benefactor. Melville sees him again on his return and "affectionately" dedicates *Typee* to him. Whom does Melville marry on August 4, 1847, three days after his twenty-eighth birthday? Is it Elizabeth Shaw? Or, in that slavish veneration which binds him to several father-images and everything that pertains to them, Judge Shaw's daughter? One wonders.

While Melville was pursuing fabulous dragons across the vacant seas, America had been awakening, growing aware of itself, leaving behind its long, childhood torpor. Belated, floundering among the inhibitions of a bourgeoisie even more philistine than puritanical, and yet vigorous, American romanticism is in full swing when our sailor returns home. Edgar Allan Poe has been living in New York since 1844. In 1845 he published *The Raven*, which has made him almost famous. He is on the fringes of all that is specifically American in this movement. His symbols are opaque and shrink from any allegorical interpretation. Yet he has written *The Narrative of A. Gordon Pym* in 1838 and in 1841, *A Descent into the Maelstrom*. The influence of both will be felt strongly in *Moby Dick*, especially in the final section.

A little to the north of the country of the Gansevoorts, not far from Boston, is the inspired village of Concord, the center of what F. O. Matthiessen calls the "American Renaissance."* In Concord lives Emerson. In 1836 he published *Nature*. In 1837, before the students of Harvard, he pronounced "our intellectual Declaration of Independence," as Oliver Wendell Holmes will call it. In 1841 he published, among other essays, "The Oversoul," which is central to his doctrine. There is a world-spirit, a spirit of the whole, but each individual soul is identical with that world-soul whose movements it reflects and reproduces. The cruel, hidden arbitrary God of the Calvinists, replaced by this luminous immanence, this participation in the Divine, is to become a splendid principle of exaltation. Beside Emerson we find Thoreau, who edits *The Dial* with him, then passes two years of almost total

---

* F.O. Matthiessen, *American Renaissance*, Oxford University Press, N.Y., 1949.

solitude in the hermitage which he built for himself near Walden Pond, lost in contemplation of Nature, or rather in a mystic participation with it, absorbing the feeling of the growth of trees and the rhythm of the clouds and the memory of the earth. The Transcendentalists, more or less grouped around Emerson, are preaching a mystic individualism in which the very element of refusal of Society is integrated, thanks to a triumphant dialectic, in the reaffirmation of a humanity sure of its values and of the infinitude of its possibilities. From across the Atlantic Emerson carries on a dialogue with Carlyle and with German thought. The air is full of rustlings and rumors, of great ambitions and exalted ideas. All literary creation is affected by it. Through the use of symbols, the slightest story can call first principles into question. Beside the Concord River, on the edge of Transcendentalism, Nathaniel Hawthorne tranquilly puts the doctrine to his own uses. In 1846 he is forty-two and has published his *Twice Told Tales* and more recently, *Mosses from an old Manse*.

Who could doubt that the young writer Herman Melville would not be moved in turn by this great wave of spiritual discovery? His relations with Transcendentalism and with Emerson in particular will be ambivalent to say the least, but we shall see how his

Thoreau in traveling clothes.

furiously nonconformist, cosmic vision falls within the great circle; how his symbolism links him in spite of himself to this young tradition. But it takes many more things than ideas to make up the intellectual life of any given period. There are the men, who, by their prestige, help the ideas to defend and propagate themselves, who form what was to be known, far from New York, as the intelligentsia. His having written *Typee* and *Omoo* was going to put Melville in contact with ideas and with intellectuals; contacts which would both help and hurt him.

It was Evert Duyckinck, editor of *Putnam's Library of Choice Reading* and, more important, of one of the first American literary reviews, the *Literary World*, who was the chief intermediary between Melville and the intellectuals. *Typee* appeared in the *Library*, and Melville was a regular contributor to the *Literary World*. Duyckinck introduced him to literary people, men of letters, artists. If we agree in attributing a vital importance in Melville's development to certain cruel complexes, it may be of some interest to know what opinion this friend and benefactor had of his young protégé. We can glimpse it in a letter of Duyckinck to Hawthorne dated March 13, 1846, in which he tells him of *Typee*, "a frenchy colored picture of the Marquesan islanders":

Emerson as a lecturer.

(the word frenchy, which will later on be applied to *La Vie Pari-sienne*, is in itself an indication of Duyckinck's opinion). "It's a lively and pleasant book," concludes Duyckinck, "Not over-philosophical, perhaps."

This benevolent and condescending judgment seems, to me at least, typical of what led Melville on from *Omoo* to *Mardi*. And, after all, had the success of *Typee* and *Omoo* really been enough to satisfy a proud, turbulent spirit like Melville's? People said: "Amazing that a sailor could do it. Amazing, if it's true." And Melville, in his humiliated pride, could well ask himself whether he was a celebrity or a curiosity. Melville, with the self-taught writer's reverence for ideas, might well ask himself whether he was going to recognize that other Melville, that invention of a fickle, superficial public whom he had helped to betray so completely, that which he was already beginning to feel seethe within him in that early stage of his "development." He had more or less consciously imagined that he had been admitted to that romantic class of the men of genius, the high priests of the new era. A sailor among cannibals? That, after all, was what it all amounted to! No doubt it was in this frame of mind that he began a third book about the South seas. In his correspondence he hints that it will be different from the others. He says that he feels "an incurable disgust" for factual truth. When he related facts, people suspected him of inventing them; they imagined that his genius was of a mediocre kind. Warming to the game, he decided to write a real novel this time. In a short preface to the published version he calculates ironically the reactions of his readers, and wonders whether, now that he has written a novel, people will take it for a factual account. There was, alas, little chance of this.

He wants to show also the "poetic" possibilities the Polynesian raw material can assume in his hands. He writes to his editor, as the young Milton wrote to his friend Diodati, that his genius is resolutely preparing its wings for flight. But let there be no mistaking the nature of his exaltation: it is that of a fever rather than of joy.

Indeed, during the writing of *Mardi* Melville cut himself off from the happiness of a normal life, choosing the lot of the solitary, accursed writer, impoverished because he will not bow to the tastes of the public. Later on his wife will write in a biography of him that during the winter of 1847 and 1848 he worked without a fire, bundled up in a freezing cold room, as he will describe

Pierre working later on: "Ah, shivering thus day after day in his wrappers and cloaks, is this the warm lad that once sung to the world of the Tropical Summer?"

Material discomfort is only a symptom, cultivated beyond what was necessary with a masochistic insistence. Note with what a heavy heart Melville annotates Seneca's *Morals* while he is writing *Mardi*. He shares in all glorification of suffering, choosing it as a means of self-discovery. And we witness a strange and painful second birth: angel, sinner, damned soul, Melville casts himself from Eden and goes to spend a long season in hell.

The man who thus thrusts himself into solitude and tragedy is a "young husband." Elizabeth Melville did not count for much in these choices and attitudes, this behavior which must have affected her with painful directness. Pierre will treat her his fictional counterpart, the pale Lucy Tarton, with a mixture of resentment and tender remorse.

It should be added that there exists simultaneously with this solitary and morose figure another Melville, a Melville for the others, who still acts as people expect him to, a jolly fellow, full of vitality, the author of *Typee*. On October 13, 1849, N. P. Willis describes him in the *New York Home Journal*: "Herman Melville, with his cigar and his Spanish eyes, *talks* Typee and Omoo, just as you find the flow of his delightful mind on paper. Those who have only read his books know the man – those who have only seen the man have a fair idea of his books." And Sophia Hawthorne, the following year, will be struck by the vitality of the man she calls Mr. Omoo, by his physical vigor, by the talent for mimicry that he shares with all the great imaginative geniuses, to the point where she succumbs to the contagion and looks about for the imaginary club with which he has just fought the Kanakas. One is tempted to believe that the Melville of Sophia, Willis, and all those who met him at that time was originally no less real than the other. Only it ceases gradually to be so, because, more and more, Melville's conscience renounces it and in some way starves it to death, while it nourishes the other Melville, the somber, brooding one.

Then everything becomes revelation and upheaval. Melville is an adult who is learning to read. He finds an edition of Shakespeare with print large enough for his sensitive and chronically tired eyes, and reads it through: "I have lived more than twenty-nine years, and until a few days ago, never made close acquaintances with the divine William. Ah, he's full of sermons-on-the-mount, and gentle, aye, almost as Jesus. I take such men to be inspired... if another Messiah ever comes 'twill be in Shakespeare's person."

From the passages he underlines and the commentaries he adds, we see that it is the bitter, despairing aspect of the author of *Measure for Measure, Lear,* and *Timon of Athens* that he understands most naturally. When *Mardi* is about to be published in London, Herman asks John Murray not to call him "the author of *Typee* and *Omoo.*" And he will write in *Pierre*, apropos of the sudden success of young writers: "It will be almost invariably observable, that for that instant success they were chiefly indebted to some rich and peculiar experience in life, embodied in a book, which because, for that cause, contained original matter, the author himself, forsooth, is to be considered original." Melville no longer wants to owe anything to the accidental happenings of his life, to the picturesque peculiarities of his experience: he wants to be read for himself and not for his cannibals.

Thus a kind of complex began to grow up within him, against the background of the immense pride which he was to assume and then denounce, as his main characteristic, in *Pierre*. He rejects the universe of *Typee* and *Omoo* absolutely and in all its aspects. He rejects the inventor with the invention, considering the whole as superficial, inferior, and vulgar. He has absorbed culture with that morbid hunger which, be it physical or mental, is a sign of anxiety. Never, perhaps, did a man feel so profoundly stirred by merely the books he read, nor seize them as realities to such an extent. Beyond the great books he glimpsed a sudden terrifying vision of himself, the feeling that he had never known himself before. He is haunted, and we shall hear him speak, like a fabulous ventriloquist, with the voice and the very inflections of Shakespeare, Sir Thomas Browne, or Carlyle. He managed to escape himself only to fall into a strange separation from reality, whose consequences for both the man and his thinking will be profound, and whose influence on the writer will be marked by the combination of an intense, unbalanced subjectivity, with composite means of expression.

For those who wish to understand Melville, *Mardi* is a key. If it seems to begin in the same way as the previous books, we know nonetheless that, from the very beginning, Melville's intentions were different. Embarked this time on a real novel, in which his imagination could have free play, he was first of all going to prove through contrast the truth of the two previous tales; secondly he was going to force the public to recognize in him a true writer, a poet, a thinker. Thus the artist begins his picture differently. Instead of narrating, he composes; instead of following the data furnished by his memories, he creates symbols: he speaks of sharks as he will speak later on of the whale. Moved by a kind of inner necessity, his imagination goes off in a direction it has taken before, obeying an instinctive reflex of his body and soul: that of escape, of flight. To desert, to flee the ship. This time it happens in mid-ocean, and we should note here a more or less conscious desire to lose himself far more completely than in *Typee*, among the cannibals.

But exactly where and how does Melville envision the rest of his novel? Determined to amuse himself no longer, hemmed in as he was by egotism and innocent of literature, what kind of a novel structure could he hope to build? Obviously he was in search of symbolism. For lack of having sufficiently thought out the role which his own experience was to play, he fell a prey to allegory.

A highly traditional childhood daydream of erotic glory introduces a beautiful female captive into the tale, ready and waiting to be saved by a heroic intervention. Thus Melville's affective immaturity is obvious from the beginning in his choice of such a theme. The narrator's crew meets a canoe in which an old Polynesian priest is leading to the sacrifice a frail blonde virgin who is as completely as possible *a foreigner*. It is here that our young Calvinist comes into his heritage of guilt. To save Yillah, the hero kills the priest. The Ancient Mariner was not more accursed for having killed the albatross. Doubtless the destructive act here is much more complex: it implicates and irreparably wounds the victim who is saved in order that she may be possessed.

Proud of his victory for the moment, the hero docks at the archipelago of Mardi, where he is mistaken for the demigod Tadji, and received, regaled, and honored as such: the former captive of *Typee* gets his revenge. But at this moment Yillah disappears. Her pursuit becomes the principal event in the book, but Yillah is no longer able to pass as a woman, a flesh and blood creature. She has become an idea, a symbol of spiritual beauty, of harmony, of purity. The story will develop only in terms of allegory, as *Pilgrim's Progress* narrates the adventures of the soul in quest of supreme goodness.

The naive author puts before us, by means of tales, fables, and symbols, all the great questions of metaphysics and ethics, as if they had not already gone into retirement in treatises and manuals. It seems as though he had wanted to cram all the speculations on time and eternity, the finite and the infinite, mind and matter, as well as those concerning human societies into this fat work, on which he lavished humor, verve, imagination, irony, and eloquence, without however succeeding in making the heavy dough rise.

Much more than the author of *Typee*, the author of *Mardi* is dual. The rationalist, the "philosopher" (in the eighteenth-century European sense), the friend-to-man is always there. But Emersonian transcendentalism, the prevailing national spirit, has infused into it some pantheistic exaltation, some aroma of mysticism, perhaps that of a mystique of humanity. Melville salutes "the great democracy of men of all classes."

The transcendentalist influence: Concord.

The cannibalistic obsession.

In real life he doesn't forget so easily that sailors are not sons of gentlemen, but here he proclaims, as he will in all his succeeding works, the brotherhood of individuals and races: "The New Zealander's tattooing is not a prodigy; nor the Chinaman's way an enigma. No custom is strange, no creed is absurd; no foe but who will in the end prove a friend."

The earth is a living cosmos: "All are parts of One. . . . Who is this? – a God? What a lake-like brow! Transparent as the morning air! I see his thoughts like worlds revolving, and in his eyes like unto heavens soft falling stars are shooting."

Nonetheless, Melville hardly succeeds in making this Emersonian soul – delivered from the infernal solitude of sin and the ego, communicating with the All, the One – his own, nor will he try to again.

53

In his more lighthearted days he could play at being a free-thinker. Here he is already a Christian in revolt, and he will remain so until the reconciliation of *Billy Budd*. He is the enemy of priests, sects, and their cruel oppressions. But his mind is not satisfied by the cynical, bitter negations which he puts in the mouth of a familiar demon. As a matter of fact, Babbalanja, who is Melville the thinker, abandons the vain quest to Serenia; in other words he reposes in the Christian idea of a principle of universal love whose affirmation remains surrounded by mystery, sadness and terror, since it must take death into account. "Beatitude there is none. Great love is sad and heaven is love. Sin is death. Why create the seeds of sin and suffering but to perish?"

This somber Christianity is combined with a heroic spirit of Christian brotherhood which will hear of no exception to its rule and which transposes Melville's democracy to the metaphysical level: "Better were we all annihilated than that one man be damned."

For himself, and such is indeed the illusory image of his liberty, the author pronounces: "I can most happily, or least miserably exist, by the practice of righteousness."

But as for men in general, he knows and he proclaims that none is master of his fate, and that good and evil are inextricable: "Oro is *in* all things, and himself *is* all things.... ...But since evil abounds and Oro is all things, he cannot be perfectly good."

If, in *Mardi*, the investigation of the problems of man constitutes a dead weight, the quest is, at least in principle, highly significant. Yillah, become spiritual image, expresses nevertheless by her form the impossible desire for a kind of physical possession which would leave her intact and pure. Here we find the foundations of the introversion and the morbid sexual idealism which Melville will transmit from himself to Pierre. The quest expresses an obstinate, despairing effort to recover natal or prenatal integrity, innocence in the Blakean sense.

Tadji, the Promethean, sacrilegious murderer, is without hope. Nevertheless, he is "inflexible as destiny" in his pursuit of the woman he has lost, and it is the horror of this fatality that gradually begins to fill the work. The quest becomes increasingly a flight, and symbols of flight become more and more frequent. Flight from a nameless, faceless horror, from phantoms and guilt, flight from the ineluctable shadows one carries with one. Tadji is pursued by three avengers and three temptresses. The temptresses, bearing symbolic, flowery messages are the emissaries of the dark-haired Hautia, symbol of all that is carnal, sensual, demoniac. Yet Hautia promises him Yillah and the venerable sage Mohi announces: "The maidens of Hautia are all Yillahs, held captive, unknown to themselves." In other words, it is an ideal, spiritual good that we are pursuing through the senses. But Tadji tries in vain to persuade himself of this: "As my hand touched Hautia's, down dropped a dead bird from the clouds."

The faces of the three temptresses melt and disappear into those of the three avengers: it is they who give the book its intimate, subjective meaning. After Melville's carefree, wandering sailor's life came a carefree wandering literary life. But now, almost in spite of himself, he discovers the full significance of this instinct which he had at first cast upon the sea. The picaresque ramble, the illusory liberty have become the destiny of Adam, while that of Cain, more guilty and more cruelly pursued, is described in these terms: "Foremost in the prow stood three men, their javelins poised for a dart... baying like hounds on their game. My own heart beat hard with undefinable dread. The corpse of Aleema seemed floating before, its avengers were raging behind."

Nevertheless this destiny and punishment of the guilt-ridden soul are contained in a firm spirit, scornful of ports and havens, determined to play its role to the bitter end of the fatal, sacred drama. The movement of the book would be beautiful if it were more discernable, and if it began with the idea of a voyage by dead reckoning in search of unknown islands. ("If unknowingly we should pass the spot where, according to our reckoning, our islands lay, upon what shoreless sea would we launch?") And if it had as its final proposition, this challenge: "Now, I am my soul's own emperor and my first act is abdication! Hail! realm of shades! And turning my prow into the racing tide, which seized me like a hand omnipotent, I darted through.... What may be mine, that will I endure, in its own essence to the quick. Let me feel the poniard if it stabs!"

Already the will of Ahab, the resolution of Pierre are prefigured: to discover oneself, and whatever else there may be, in the supreme encounter, the final instant of destiny and destruction.

Double "tiki" from the Marquesas Islands.

One of Gauguin's woodcuts for Noa Noa.

Model of the Acushnet.

The White Whale

Weighing Anchor

The Fortunate Isles are far behind us. With *Mardi*, the result
of a choice that is both objectively gratuitous and subjectively
necessary, Melville begins his dark hand-to-hand struggle with
what is to be henceforth for him man's one reality: evil and
suffering. At any rate, in consecrating himself as a writer to the
discovery of our condition, Melville envisaged a good in proportion to the severe dignity of his mission.

It was one of the great illusions of his life, and it was followed
by one of the most violent disappointments.

Mardi produced a kind of a daze in the literary world and among
the reading public, which we can understand if we remember that
Melville had begun tagged as a sea-wolf, and was expected to
produce lusty yarns in the manner of *Typee*. The failure of *Mardi*
was due to the refusal of critics and public to recognize the true
Melville. His observations in his London journal (1850) already
point to the obstinacy of his despair: "...A hollow purse makes
the poet *sink* – witness *Mardi*. But we that write & print
have all our books predestinated – & for me, I shall write such
things as the Great Publisher of Mankind ordained ages before
he published the world – this planet, I mean.... ...What a madness & anguish it is, that an author can never – under no conceivable circumstances – be at all frank with his readers."

59

One must make a living, play the part of the old salt, and write *Redburn*. It is because he cannot do otherwise that Melville infuses this neglected tale so profoundly with his obsessions: the theme of the green jacket, a garment of derision and humiliation; the theme of the orphan's quest for the father or for his image; the related themes of death, sin, and evil.

The feeling of death is everywhere and takes on multiple forms. The first is that of drowning. The ship is scarcely at sea before Redburn sees in a flash of lightning a madman rush on deck and leap into the sea. This apparently happened in 1839 and Melville is recounting it in 1848. But in a few months, in October, 1849, he will take passage on a ship bound for England and his journal will tell how an insane passenger jumped overboard and allowed himself to sink rather than to be saved, with a kind of defiant, mocking smile, as though he knew some secret he refused to tell. Obviously this must have been an astounding scene to witness. Melville, recounting the episode in his journal, appears absolutely unaware that he had already invented a similar scene a few months earlier in *Redburn*, or that he had witnessed another such incident ten years earlier. This repetition, together with the drowning which he will add just for good measure to *White Jacket* (nor is there any lack of drownings in *Mardi*, for that matter) suggests a strange obsession, and makes us wonder whether a kind of hallucinatory vision was not engendered in his mind at the very sight of the sea. Before his death, the suicide in *Redburn* (writes Melville) "had been occupying the very bunk which I had appropriated for myself, and there was no other place for me to sleep in."

Thus, to the detriment of the probability of his tale, he affirms his identity with death; he has committed a symbolic suicide.

He imbues himself with death as did the German romantics with whom he has many points in common – with its most hideously material and tangible aspects, but also with death as an *apparition*: one day at sea they come upon a drifting hulk manned by three corpses – "three dark, green, grassy objects...."

On the return voyage a sailor whom the crew imagines is drunk but who is actually dead is kidnapped onto the *Highlander*, to be pressed into service. And when night falls, Melville regales us with a bravura passage: "...Two threads of greenish fire, like a forked tongue, darted out between the lips; and in a moment the cadaverous face was crawled over by a swarm of worm-like flames.... ...Covered all over with spires and sparkles of flame that faintly crackled in the silence, the uncovered part of the body burned before us, precisely like phosphorescent shark in a midnight sea.... The whole face, now wound in curls of soft blue flame, wore an aspect of grim defiance and eternal death."

The look of defiant mockery, most significant among the various Melvillian attitudes, will also be that of the suicide in the journal. It is the defiance of man *whoever he may be* – the defiance of Prometheus – one of the two terms of the extremely limited dialogue which may take place between the hidden Creator and his creation. And here is the other term: "For me, who at that age had never so much as happened to hear of a case like this of animal combustion, in the horrid mood that came over me, I almost thought the burning body was a premonition of the hell of the Calvinists."

A series of identifications characterizes Melville's imagination. Just as he here identifies himself with the dead man, so elsewhere he identifies himself with the sin whose reward is death. The escapade at London with his handsome friend Harry Bolton is a curious episode with a symbolism close to that of Hawthorne's in *The Blithedale Romance*, which Melville has not yet come upon. The scene takes place entirely at night. The two men arrive in London at night and leave it by night, like blindfolded prisoners; and the city is merely a phantom surrounding a luxurious palace of vice. Bolton disappears, leaving his friend prisoner of an infernal, luminous solitude in which valets pass to and fro amid marble and mirrors. A palace of Eblis (the image is Melville's), worthy of Beckford, whose marble flagstones echo hollowly, whose perspectives are all in *trompe l'oeil*, whose lewd paintings agitate the guilty, puritanical imagination: "I shuddered at every footfall, and almost thought it must be some assassin pursuing me. The whole place seemed infected; and a strange thought came over me, that in the very damasks around, some eastern plague had been imported.... This must be some house whose foundations take hold on the pit.... I was mysteriously alive to a dreadful feeling, which I had never before felt, except when penetrating into the lowest and most squalid haunts of sailor iniquity in Liverpool. All the mirror and marbles around me seemed crawling over with lizards; and I thought to myself, that though gilded and golden, the serpent of vice is a serpent still."

Nothing in this episode is more striking than the hero's strict confinement, the impossibility of contact with the outside world. When later on he writes the biography of Israel Potter, that unlucky soldier in the American Revolution, Melville will show him

ISRAEL R. POTTER,

at Franklin's home in Paris, imprisoned in the midst of a forbidden city, just as Redburn is here.

The Palace of Aladdin is more than a symbolic shell. Evil, seen as a metaphysical principle in a system tending towards Manicheism – as often with the Romantics – is personified by the sailor Jackson. He "seemed to be full of hatred and gall against everything and everybody in the world," as if the whole world were a person who had inflicted some frightful wrong on him. He is "spontaneously an atheist and infidel." He sees "nothing to be loved, and nothing worth living for but everything to be hated in the wide world." He is Cain, "branded on his yellow brow with some inscrutable curse." His misanthropic soul is exasperated to the point of madness. He is visibly a prey to "unspeakable mental terrors only known to the damned on earth." He seems "determined to die with a curse on his teeth," as he will, as a matter of fact, do, when after having spat out that curse with the blood of his lungs, he plummets from the rigging straight down into the engulfing sea. ". . . This Jackson's would have been the face [for Salvatore Rosa] to paint for the doomed vessel's figurehead, seamed and blasted by lightning."

Note the presence of lightning, and note how Jackson is the dissolute brother, but the brother of the noble Ahab. In Melville's unconscious the end of the *Pequod* – sunk by the whale Moby Dick but even more surely by its own Captain Ahab, and going down in a whirlpool – is already conceived and linked to a diabolical will. Let us note too his powerful, essentially poetic spouting forth of images which will remain at the gateway of consciousness until they have been completely and adequately formulated, until they have accomplished their destiny as symbols. Because of this necessity the character of Jackson prefigures the condemned vessel in *Benito Cereno* with its skeleton in the prow, as it also prefigures Ahab in its body torn apart by lightning and its diabolical will bearing the terrible force which will engulf the ship and its men.

But this first sketch is a rough one. The damned soul is finally only a poor devil. For Melville hasn't yet chosen revolt. He has not taken the responsibility of Jackson upon himself. If he compares this Yankee hoodlum to Tiberius, it is because, he immediately adds, there is in any case "no dignity in wickedness." Without Milton, Satan would be admired only by "pickpockets and burglars." Melville's voice is still that of the gentleman's son.

Thus it was in spite of himself that Melville, like a true romantic, associated evil with energy and influence. Lacking physical force and already singled out by death, Jackson exerts a terrible, inexplicable authority over the rest of the crew. He remains anecdotal and without power over the collective destiny, but Melville has tried to describe a direct relationship between the narrator and the demon. Jackson considers Redburn his personal enemy; as a result, Redburn says: "I found myself a sort of Ishmael in the ship, without a single friend or companion; and I began to feel a hatred growing up in me against the whole crew...." One can see in this feeling the primitive autobiographical reality of Ishmael. In *Moby Dick*, where all memory is entirely subjected to an imagination sure of its means and its ends, the humble figure of Ishmael balances the ferocious, destructive grandeur of Ahab, formulating gradually the principle of love and reconciliation.

In contrast to *Redburn*, *White Jacket* presents not only symbolic themes, but also a suggestion of total symbolism. The frigate *Neversink* is an image of humanity. It has secret orders, as humanity in the author's Calvinist vision had an unknown but predetermined fate. Note the insistence of the motifs of predestination and their weight of sadness. The character's names are labels, and point to the absence of moral autonomy. Bland, the master-at-arms, a suave, likable, fearless rascal, sure of finding friends and accomplices everywhere, is "an organic scoundrel." But what responsibility, in that case, can be imputed to him? Proceeding from the Calvinist idea that everyone is guilty, Melville has begun groping toward the idea – and it is in this that he is truly "democratic" – that no one is guilty. In this new perspective he will more and more begin to side with the victims. Melville wrote two successive books in order to earn a living – that is, in humiliation. Sickened by the relationship between the writer and his public, he is once again seized by an urge to flee. He finds a reason for leaving – he will go to London to look for a publisher for *White Jacket*. Notwithstanding moments of humor and malicious verve, what strikes us most as we read his journal is the lack of *vital* contact with the reality he describes. The traveler carries his customary symbols – a jacket (green, this time) that causes people to turn and stare at him – and seizes the substance of future symbols as they pass.

It is on Melville's return (we are now in February, 1850) that he begins to read the Bible, underlining the sublime and the somber passages. He turns to the Book of Job. "Canst thou draw out leviathan with an hook?" And he begins planning *Moby Dick*.

A new influence now began to take hold of Melville's imagination – that of Hawthorne. In the spring of 1850, Melville read *The Scarlet Letter*. The effect on him was one of veritable possession – not that of a book, but that of a man. Melville is fascinated, bewitched. "A man of a deep & noble nature has seized me in this seclusion. His wild, witch voice rings thro' me...."

He then reads *Mosses from an old Manse*, and writes an essay on his hero which is published anonymously. He salutes in him the American, the Puritan, the man who can look straight at "the darkness and decay and inscrutable malevolence of the universe." And he discovers at last another writer beside himself who is trying to get at the very heart of things. "Now, it is that blackness in Hawthorne, of which I have spoken, that so fixes and fascinates me. It may be, nevertheless, that it is too largely developed in him. Perhaps he does not give us a ray of light for every shade of his dark. But however this may be, this blackness is that which furnishes the infinite depths of his background...." He compares Hawthorne to Shakespeare, to Shakespeare at his most somber, who deserved "the loftiest but must circumscribed renown." "Through the mouths of the dark characters of Hamlet, Timon, Lear, and Iago, he craftily says, or sometimes insinuates the things which we feel to be so terrifically true, that it were all but madness for any good man, in his own proper character, to utter, or even hint of them. Tormented into desperation, Lear, the frantic king, tears off the mask & speaks the sane madness of vital truth."

Now Melville knows what he wants to do, what he will attempt in *Moby Dick* and in *Pierre*: to tear off the mask, to give utterance to these lucid ravings. These men and books whom he takes up so eagerly are precisely those which seem to hold the key to himself.

Longfellow and Hawthorne read with delight the anonymous article – the first in which Hawthorne was understood, and Sophia Hawthorne in one of her letters wonders "who can he be, so fearless, so rich in heart, of such fine intuition?" In the next line she mentions Melville's books; Hawthorne in turn speaks in a letter of the richness of *Mardi*, with its "depths here and there that compel a man to swim for his life." He goes on to mention the two articles on himself by an unknown author.

By September, 1850, Hawthorne and Melville are friends and neighbours, Melville having bought a farm near Pittsfield. Sophia writes of "Mr. Omoo": "We find him... earnest, sincere & reverent, very tender & *modest* – And I am not sure that he is not a very great man.... He seems to see everything very accurately, & how he can do so with his small eyes, I cannot tell.... He is tall & erect with an air free, brave, & manly.... There is no grace,

65

nor polish – once in a while, his animation gives place to a singularly quiet expression... an indrawn, dim look, but which at the same time makes you feel that he is at that instant taking the deepest note of what is before him. It is a strange, lazy glance but with a power that is quite unique – it does not seem to penetrate through you, but to take you into himself."

Thus, while Melville is engaged in writing *Moby Dick* he lives a period of intense personal relationships. His almost deliriously exalted feelings must have sometimes embarrassed the grave and placid Nathaniel: "I feel that the Godhead is broken up like the bread at the Supper, and that we are the pieces.... Hence this infinite fraternity of feeling.... Knowing you persuades me more than the Bible of our immortality."

Never, one feels, was a man so in need of mediating saints in order to feel that he existed. And he had found one at last. In April, 1851, Melville read a copy of *The House of the Seven Gables* which Hawthorne had given him. And he writes to him: "There is a certain tragic phase of humanity which, in our opinion, was never more powerfully embodied than by Hawthorne. We mean the tragicness of human thought in its own unbiassed, native, and profounder workings. We think that into no recorded mind has the intense feeling of the visible truth ever entered more deeply than into this man's. By visible truth, we mean the apprehension of the absolute condition of present things as they strike the eye of the man who fears them not, though they do their worst to him.... There is the grand truth about Nathaniel Hawthorne. He says NO! in thunder; but the devil himself cannot make him say *yes*. For all men who say *yes*, lie; and all men who say *no*, – why, they are in the happy condition of judicious, unencumbered travellers in Europe; they cross the frontiers into Eternity with nothing but a carpet-bag, – that is to say, the Ego."

Meanwhile "Mr. Omoo" subsists. He has, it seems, changed his career as a seaman for that of a farmer. He writes: "I rise at eight – thereabouts – and go to my barn – say good-morning to the horse, and give him his breakfast. (It goes to my heart to give him a cold one, but it can't be helped.) Then, pay a visit to my cow – cut up a pumpkin or two for her, and stand by to see her eat it – for it's a pleasant sight to see a cow move her jaws – and she does it so mildly and with such a sanctity." But it is not certain that his bucolic day didn't end with the animal's breakfast. Melville was never really a farmer. As soon as possible he would sit down before his manuscript and begin writing furiously, like a kind of barbaric Flaubert. According to his wife he used to remain seated all day at his desk until four or five in the afternoon without eating. Only when night forced him to leave off working would he get up; his eyesight had been weakened by scarlet fever, and he could not bear to work by lamplight.

He wrote without being able to forget that he was a poor, obscure writer. "Dollars damn me.... What I feel most moved to write – that is banned, – it will not pay. Yet, altogether, write the *other* way I cannot. So the product is a final hash, and all my books are botches." The terrible pride of the humiliated man tortures him, and poisons the eulogies which he receives and which are intended not for him, but for the author of his books: "My dear Sir, they begin to patronize. All Fame is patronage. Let me be infamous: there is no patronage in *that*. What reputation H.M. has is horrible. Think of it! To go down to posterity is bad enough, anyway: but to go down as a 'man who lived among cannibals!'" *Let me be infamous*: this is the key. Melville finishes his book amid torments which will be evoked later in the darkest pages of *Pierre*. In June, 1851 he goes to shut himself up in a depressing room in New York, so as to be able to start correcting as soon as the proofs are finished. But he is unable to bear this and returns to Pittsfield. At this point he writes Hawthorne a letter of which he says, not without reason: "This is rather a crazy letter in some respects, I apprehend.... Have ready a bottle of brandy, because I always feel like drinking that heroic drink when we talk ontological heroics together." He never doubts for a moment that Hawthorne does not exactly share his taste for this prodigious metaphysical mixture: there are questions which in his egotism he never asks himself. But those who know Hawthorne cannot help asking them.

The Whale

The Whale was published in London on October 18, 1851; *Moby Dick or the Whale* appeared in New York a few weeks later, with a dedication to Nathaniel Hawthorne. One wonders how Melville had managed to take a year and a half to write *Moby Dick*, after having announced in his letters soon after beginning it that he was half finished, and later that it was almost completed. It has been suggested that he quickly wrote a first version which did not satisfy him,* or which ceased to satisfy him when, in the beginning of the summer of 1850, Hawthorne's writing began to enlighten him as to what he himself wanted to do. At this point, he perhaps transformed and partly rewrote his book.

The book's composite character has been cited as an argument in favor of this hypothesis. We should note, however, that as far back as *Typee* he was oscillating from chapter to chapter between imaginative and highly factual prose; a mixture of story-telling and essay-writing characterizes *White Jacket* and *Omoo*, and *Mardi* combines all the genres. Certainly *Moby Dick* is more like one of those strange blocks of several metals melted together but nevertheless remaining distinct than like a solid, highly refined ingot. But this, after all, is typical of Melville.

If there was a recasting of the book (which to me seems problematical and which, since we do not have two texts to compare, is ultimately of little importance) Hawthorne may not have aided Melville to raise his work to the dignity of a symbolic vision as has been suggested, but instead to attenuate the allegory to which Melville was all too inclined, and to remember that reality is the living form of the symbol.

One is struck by the novel's cultural trappings; it begins with an eight-page anthology of quotations, from the Bible to Darwin, by way of Plutarch, Lucian, Pliny, Montaigne, Rabelais, Shakespeare, Sir Thomas Browne, Hobbes, Bunyan, Milton, Dryden, Ulloa, Pope, Goldsmith, Cook, Jefferson, Burke, Cuvier, Lamb, Eckermann, Goethe, Carlyle, and James Fenimore Cooper, as well as various jurists, travelers, and popular ballads. What is exactly the point of this overture, continued later on by numerous learned exposés, directly or indirectly presented?

It is a question first of all, I think, of the honor of the subject

---

* This is the hypothesis which Howard Vincent argues vigorously in his *The Trying Out of Moby Dick*.

Mocha Dick, the real whale, Moby Dick's ancestor.

matter. Melville wishes to prove that one may treat a rude subject in a noble style, to warn the reader not to expect a whaling yarn viewed from the forecastle, which would be the natural sequel to the cannibal tales – in a word, to inspire his respect.

If he affirms that the whale which has haunted men's imaginations throughout the ages, a type and symbol of the mystery of nature and the world, is not unworthy of the cultured man's attention, he implies on the other hand that culture is perhaps not a sufficient tool for grasping the magnitude of the whale, that there is something ridiculous about speculation in relation to life, reality, and mystery. One does not tame the abyss with definitions and classifications. At the very heart of the book, the chapter entitled *Cetology* bears witness to this idea again: "To have one's hands among the unspeakable foundations, ribs, and very pelvis of the world; this is a fearful thing. What am I that I should essay to hook the nose of this leviathan .... But I have swum through libraries and sailed through oceans; I have had to do with whales with these visible hands...."

And, having mockingly made this point, he sets out to *convert* his whales, render them *assimilable* to man and his libraries, classifying them by format: folio, octavo, duodecimo, and so on. But if one can really have *knowledge* of the whale, one will not find it on the shelves of a library but in a fatal encounter. Science imagines it can master reality by classifying facts. This is a ridiculous pretention. Nonetheless facts are fascinating and Melville has an insatiable curiosity. From a simple and seemingly tongue-in-cheek enumeration of the whale's various characteristics, something of the whale will come to light. Parody at first conceals a fascination and later goes thoroughly astray. The heavily disguised mannerisms in *Moby Dick* are closer to mimesis than to parody.

Instinctively an allegorist, Melville creates a whale-world and imprisons us in it. The whale is first zoological, then cosmological, then becomes the leviathan, the indomitable manifestation of God's power and will – while continuing to remain a tangible living being – through a contemplation of its infinite detail and miraculous ordering that is both minute and mystical and reminds one of the way in which Blake makes his tiger suddenly loom before us in all his fatal splendor. It is the mystery of the world rendered suddenly palpable, forcing us violently to recognize it. The *presence* of the sacred is the goal of the imagination's loftiest intuitions; it exists only in the form of a *vision*, and thus one may say that *Moby Dick* is a grand vision received by Melville. A

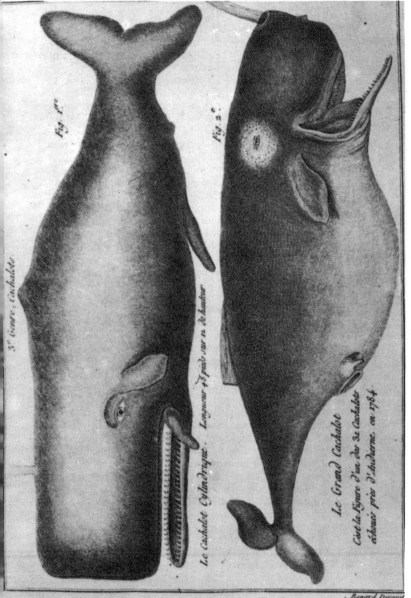

Fig. 1ᵉ

3ᵉ Genre, Cachalot.

Le Cachalot Cylindrique. Longueur 5 pieds sur 12 de hauteur.

Fig. 2ᵉ

Le Grand Cachalot

C'est la Figure d'un des 32 Cachalots échoués près d'Audierne en 1784.

Benard Direxit.

HISTOIRE NATURELLE, Cétacés.

vision which brings immensity, forever strange and yet intimately experienced, into man's very flesh, allows him to put his finger on it. Melville writes: "... It had thrice circumnavigated the globe, brushing with its flanks all the coasts of Africa...."

The whale is a symbol and is covered with symbols; it radiates unfathomable intentions: "Standing at the mast-head of my ship during a sunrise that crimsoned sky and sea, I once saw a large herd of whales in the east, all heading towards the sun, and for a moment vibrating in concert with peaked flukes. As it seemed to me at the time, such a grand embodiment of adoration of the gods was never beheld, even in Persia, the home of the fire worshippers."

Let us note in passing this whale-sun-fire relationship. The whale's universe is by no means purely aquatic. It is associated with the solar element, with the terrors of flame and the worship of fire. The whale dies facing the sun, and overwhelms Ahab himself. From chapter to chapter, it proclaims the splendor of a savage and incomprehensible universe. "Dissect him how I may, then, I but go skin deep; I know him not, and never will."

Its body is covered with hieroglyphics, but they are eternally unreadable, for life itself, or perhaps more exactly the life-force, is unintelligible.

In his thinking, Melville belongs to the great family of romantics. It was for him that Coleridge had affirmed that the poet's imagination reproduces the plasmatic force of the universe, for him that he had written *The Rime of the Ancient Mariner*, of which we find direct echoes in Melville's tale of the damned ship and the white beast, in the conception of a universe of love opposed to a universe of destruction and separation. And it is not without memories of Coleridge that Emerson constructed his philosophy on a foundation of German romanticism.

As far back as *Mardi*, Melville's relation to Emersonian thought had not been a simple one, and Emerson's pantheistic optimism will more and more infuriate Melville who *does not want* to be reassured. But it is nonetheless obvious that behind the increasing aversion a durable influence remains hidden. Emerson has a powerful sense of the cosmic. It is perhaps no coincidence that on March 3, 1849, when the grief caused by Melville's cruel separation from his public (marked by the condemnation of *Mardi*) has succeeded in forging and tempering his thinking, he associates Emerson with the whale which, oddly, already swims within him. He says of Emerson that he may be a fool but "then I had rather be a fool than a wise man... I love all men who *dive*. Any fish can swim near the surface, but it takes a great whale to go down stairs five miles or more..."

And it is doubtless no coincidence that Emerson himself takes an interest in the whales that occasionally surface in his letters: in one, dated February 19, 1834, he writes of a white whale known as Old Tom, "who rushed upon the boats which attacked him and crushed the boats to small chops in his jaws."

In another, of May 10, 1847, written from Nantucket, he evokes for his daughter the enormous cachalot which twice attacked the schooner *Essex* and sank it in a few minutes. This ferocity fascinates him, *but he is not opposed to it*. For him there is no separation between nature and us; her laws and ways, however dark and mysterious they may seem, have their correspondences in man.

Thus it is an Emersonian Melville who can write in *Moby Dick*: "O Nature and O soul of man! how far beyond all utterance are your linked analogies! not the smallest atom stirs or lives on matter, but has its cunning duplicate in mind."

Nevertheless the difference is vast, and it is characteristic of Melville. The feeling of cosmic continuity and of the meaningful texture of appearances is only one of the two terms of that dialectic. The other is the intolerable separation of that conscience within us which is in touch with nothing, not even with ourselves. Pantheism, if it does not take this reality into account, is a fraud, and how often Melville makes fun of these illusory communions!

In a letter written to Hawthorne after *Moby Dick*, he says: "You must often have felt it, lying in the grass on a warm summer's day. Your legs seem to send out shoots into the earth. Your hair feels like leaves upon your head. This is the *all* feeling. But what plays mischief with the truth is that men will insist upon the universal application of a temporary feeling or opinion."

The torment of transcendence is opposed to the peace of immanence, and the Melvillian whale is in the final analysis far from Emerson's thought. It is not merely a cosmic manifestion, not merely marked by the hand of God. It *proceeds from Him*. We must remember that Melville was immersed in the Book of Job, and especially Chapter 41, in which the terrible Leviathan is taken as the type of the terror of the living God: "None is so fierce that dare stir him up: who then is able to stand before me?"

Melville's whale is thus *angelic*: a terrible messenger of the Almighty, as he points out in the great sermon on Jonah's whale which is the real overture to the book.

But the whale comes from still farther back in the memory of

The Melvillian Leviathan.

man. This romantic notion carries us far back behind the frontiers of the rational, to a world of primitive, profound intuitions. The Melvillian Leviathan is laden with *mana*: it is more than a manifestion of God, it *is* God, just as it is terror, power, and mystery. Near the middle of the book there is a mystical apprehension of the whale, and first of all of its whiteness.

In the romantic universe of signs and symbols, whiteness occupies a choice position, and if Melville needed to follow in the footsteps of someone other than himself and his own *White Jacket*, one might imagine that he had Poe and his beautiful

tale *The Narrative of A. Gordon Pym* in mind. The latter story moves forward into a world of muffled whiteness, amid the flights of gigantic white birds, facing an enormous figure whose skin had "the perfect whiteness of snow"; after savages, to set the tone, have cried out with convulsive movements their sacred horror of everything white.

Poe blocks in his canvas with white, stepping back from time to time to admire the effect. With a completely different depth and gravity, Melville gives his whale, by means of its whiteness, an extra strangeness which renders it immediately more irreducible, a little more *foreign*. And he provides a curious analysis of this whiteness, together with a meditation interrupted by a series of visions.

To realize the peculiar effect of the whiteness, Melville dissociates and associates it by turns. In its associations with a universe of terror, whiteness is a constant: it adds a note of intensity. The white shark and the white polar bear are its prototypes. With regard to them, Melville gives a kind of poetic approximation of their quality: the clothed ferocity of white gives off a *horrible mildness*. The white whale often appears cloaked in that mildness which is to become resolutely ambiguous, equivocal. If the whiteness of these destructive creatures is terrible, it is because it is the pallor of death, the color of ghosts and shrouds, an element in all spiritual terror. It is the color of Death's horse in the Apocalypse, it is the frightening robe of the archangels. Melville establishes a continuous series of deep analogies between these foundations of our psychological world and the manifestations with which he associates them. He discovers that the French word for the (white) shark is *requin* (like *requiem*), a sign of its sinister vocation. Its livery is thus transformed into a symbolic uniform. But all this is still only the surface of the mystery, the face of horror. What are the secret connections between this definition of whiteness and the soul's terrors? Here Melville comes again upon his obsessions: white is a mask*, a false color. If white confounds all the other colors, they in their turn are only a trick and an illusion, the outward aspect of a world which is no doubt unimaginably pale and wan. Whiteness "stabs us from behind with the idea of annihilation," it is the one cruel truth behind the "subtle deceits" of colors. That indefinite tint gives us "the heartless voids and immensities of the universe." It is at once an indefinite presence and the presentiment of absence. A Pascalian dizziness forces Melville to pin down these visions, to encounter the milky way in the night sky. Whiteness is the "colorless all-color of atheism." A quasi-animal instinct allows those whose minds are not too caught up in the world to be closed to its mysteries to see this, because it permits them to glimpse "the demonism in the world."

We do not actually know which phase of this oscillation constitutes the worst terror for Melville; whether he does not prefer this demonism to the possibility of mere absence.

It seems to us today natural for Melville to have exalted his

---

* In the Chinese theater, the white mask is the mask of lies and falsehoods.

extraordinary prey. But at the time he wrote *Moby Dick* it was more than a piece of audacity, it was a daring wager. Once more, as had been the case when *Mardi* was published, he was almost certain of finding merely ridicule in his search for the sublime. He accepts this risk with the heroic and somber mood we find in his letters. The whale had to turn back into Leviathan in order for the whale-hunt to be worth his while as a writer.

Drawing of a whaling ship on whale bone.

In the South

W. B. S. B.

Ahab

No one will ever know exactly how *Moby Dick* was written. In the book which has come down to us, which is the only one we have, Melville's mixed and conflicting intentions are not easy to unravel: for example, the epic tone (a universally accepted convention) of the temptation to parody (a more dubious convention) and of the idea of the real greatness of modern man (proposition of a new truth). Affirmation of human valiance, a lament for nature, despoiled and destroyed by man? Or challenge flung at God and his nature by conquered but indomitable man, Promethean and Satanic? In some places the book is Homeric and traditional, in others Blakean and Miltonic, Christian and anti-Christian. Elsewhere it is modern in its very refusal of human enterprise, modern like Faulkner's *The Bear:* and its subject seems to be the mysterious opposition of man and a world of which he is never master. On the one hand we perceive honor between hunter and hunted, mutual respect, even fraternity, and religious gratitude for common membership in the world, for mutual responsibility, for the obligation to play one's role in the sacred drama which they stage together. On the other hand it is possible to see restlessness, shame at human avidity, at man's violation of the world, of the threat he constitutes to all that is sacred. If this were all, Moby Dick would be the only hero: on the side of the humans we should find only Ahab's first mate, some noble and valiant Starbuck. The peculiar vision of the author of *Mardi* necessarily brought into play a hero who is more personally tragic, more singularly accursed.

Between Homer and Melville there is Milton and the medieval, Neoplatonic, English conception of an epic of the soul. Milton used Satan as the protagonist of an action which was an attack on the soul. It is Ahab who bestows personality on the whale, which is by no means a terrible white whale for everyone. It becomes Evil and the Enemy in a Manichean universe only because Ahab has taken up his position opposite it to give it a personality: because what it represents becomes the object of a violent crisis of conscience and collides with the principle of pride and refusal, which is Ahab.

Since *Mardi* Melville had been a symbolist who wrote with a symbolist's memory. In the symbolist vision, where eternal figures become human for a moment of time, pass to and fro, Ahab, the Quaker captain, is also by extension Ahab, king of Israel, who did more to provoke the wrath of God than all the kings who had

Detail from the logbook of a whaling ship.

preceded him. Even before he exists for us, his name manifests a heroic, sacreligious defiance. Thus, basically, he represents pride. Isn't it in this that he is a "projection" of Melville himself? "I never yet saw him kneel," says one of the men of him. And he himself says, "I'd strike the sun if it insulted me."

He accomplishes his duties as captain haughtily, meditating in the solitude of the poop-deck, between the sea and the sky. He pits himself against the mastery of the world, a passionately religious spirit, right up to his refusal of God. He is a somber hero, ravaged, gnawed by doubt. "He looked like a man cut away from the stake, when the fire has overrunningly wasted all the limbs without consuming them.... Threading its way out from among his gray hairs, and continuing right down one side of his tawny scorched face and neck, till it disappeared in his clothing, you saw a slender rod-like mark, lividly whitish. It resembled that perpendicular seam sometimes made in the straight, lofty trunk of a great tree, when the upper lightning tearingly darts down it ... leaving the tree still greenly alive, but branded."

This haughty man is humiliated; his integrity has been violated by the *cachalot*'s terrible jaw. Melville rightly spends much time in setting the stage for his tragic hero's entrance. He is presented twice: first by Captain Peleg, then by Elijah. Peleg says, "He's a grand, ungodly, godlike man.... I know that on the passage home, he was a little out of his mind for a spell; but it was the sharp shooting pains in his bleeding stump that brought that about.... I know, too, that ever since he lost his leg last voyage by that accursed whale, he's been a kind of moody – desperate moody, and savage sometimes...." And the strange character named Elijah, like the prophet who had cursed King Ahab, adds many other details to the picture: "...that thing that happened to him off Cape Horn, long ago, when he lay like dead for three days and three nights: ... that deadly scrimmage with the Spaniard afore the altar in Santa ... [and] the silver calabash he spat into...." All this points clearly to a sacrilege. But when Elijah comes to the missing leg and insists heavily on it, the offended narrator interrupts: "I know all about the loss of his leg." And Elijah sneers: "*All* about it, eh – sure you do? – all?"

This is perhaps the most mysterious passage in the book, that which most piques the curiosity, that which has been least explained by the critics, although psychoanalytically-minded critics have as a matter of fact suggested that Captain Ahab's amputation was a physical or psychic castration. Elijah's words seem to indicate something of this sort, and are perhaps confirmed by a passage in Chapter CVI 'Ahab's Leg' which states that one day at Nantucket his ivory leg had come loose and almost pierced him in the groin: "nor was it without extreme difficulty that the agonizing wound was entirely cured."

This seems a clear indication of the subject that seems strangely to haunt Melville's imagination here. When Ahab nails to the mast the Ecuadorian doubloon ornamented with a design of three mountains ("and on the third a crowing cock") and with the signs of the Zodiac; and when Queequeg squints at the signs on his own body ("he's found something there in the vicinity of his thigh – I guess it's Sagittarius, or the Archer," says Ahab) one cannot shut one's eyes to the sexual motivation, or separate it absolutely from Ahab's madness, dissociate from a supreme humiliation that unatonable pain he feels, that suffering which inspires Melville to see "a crucifixion in his face." It is, in any case, a despair of ever existing which leaves intact only the "mechanical humming of the wheels of his vitality in him."

Just as he turned his whale into a mythological creature, Melville builds up his hunter into a colossal romantic hero. But Melville went beyond the pale, and he writes near the beginning of the book: "All mortal grandeur is but disease." Ahab is a madman, or at any rate a monomaniac, in our language; in Melville's he is a man possessed. He has the necessary wiles that the madman uses to conceal his madness so as not to jeopardize his goals. He is like a madman in his absolute inflexibility joined to a frightful lucidity; for he is well aware that the ferocious will he manifests comes not from him, that he is *under orders*, the fatal agent of a predestined action: an acute Calvinism is discernible behind this "madness." If one is tempted to speak of possession, it is because Melville does not confine us to the realm of psychology. Ahab is the term, foreseen by Melville, of a religious passion divorced from all happiness in belief and ruined by a quasi-schizophrenic isolation from the world; but he is also the human soul invaded by something unknown, external to it, by Evil as *intention*. Melville shares in this possession, or cruelly forces himself to participate in it: "Often, when forced from his hammock by exhausting and intolerably vivid dreams of the night, which, resuming his own intense thoughts through the day, carried them on amid a clashing of frenzies, and whirled them round and round in his blazing brain, till the very throbbing of his life-spot became insufferable anguish: and when, as was sometimes the case, these spiritual throes in him heaved his being up from its base, and a chasm seemed opening in him, from which forked flames and lightnings shot up, and accursed fiends beckoned him to leap down among them; when this hell in himself yawned beneath him, a wild cry would be heard through the ship; and with glaring eyes Ahab would burst from his state room, as though escaping from a bed that was on fire." The Ahab rising in terror from his hammock is not the mad, sly, implacably obstinate hunter who lay down to sleep there. The new agent is "the living principle or soul in him." Sleep having dissociated it from the idea that enslaved it, this soul "spontaneously sought escape from the scorching contiguity of the frantic thing, of which, for the time, it was no longer an integral." Elsewhere too, like Marlowe's Dr. Faustus, damned already and tortured in this world, Ahab utters "a terrific, loud, animal sob, like that of a heart-stricken moose."

The horrors of Kurtz's agony in Conrad's *Heart of Darkness* are already present here. Amid an "infinite suffering," with an "infinity of courage," which he possesses in common with Milton's Satan, Ahab is on his feet, in action. But not as a free agent – like an instrument, as Melville says. It is this fixity, this callousness stronger than the will of his basically generous nature that becomes dramatically evident when Ahab refuses to participate in the hunt for the lost son of the captain of the *Rachel*.

I am not fond of everything in *Moby Dick*. Melville accomplished in it what he had failed to do in *Mardi*, but not completely: the tremendous effort he made to project his own experiences and torments into the great myths of our culture is not always successful. Ahab issues forth from a vision of man among men and in the universe which Shakespeare illuminated for us, but just because of this he sometimes poses and spouts tirades like a tragic actor. Like every Faustian character, this Faust must have his Mephistopheles. Thus, perhaps under the influence of De Quincey's *Confessions of an English Opium Eater*, and of the dreamlike character of the Malayan, Melville flanked his captain with a Parsee who is thoroughly evil but even more unreal than supernatural. His acolytes are as gauche as certain similar characters in the work of Melville's friend Hawthorne. Their only interest is in their linking of Ahab to the cult of fire, which is for Melville's Judaized conscience the archetype of abominations and sacrileges, for it renews the worship of Baal. In order that he

Illustration from Browne's Whaling Cruise,
one of the sources of Moby Dick.

may plumb the depths of the experience of impiety and defiance, Melville imagines the diabolical ritual of the baptism of the harpoons in blood, enacted by the three infidel harpooners: "Ego non baptizo te in nomine patris sed in nomine diaboli."

What does Ahab want, and what does Melville want? And why does he need a devil to chase the white whale? It is perhaps to show that he doesn't accept the order of the world as it is, nor the role of disorder included in that order, which has come to banish it. In sealing his pact, he declares his rebellion. More specifically, what he wants, first of all, above all, is to understand what is happening to him, and hence to understand the Being from which everything proceeds. Through the narrow and limited range of his vengeance, he is seeking an absolute: he rejects along with the sextant the bonds of human knowledge, in which we never come upon anything but ourselves. Finally, he wants to *communicate*, to force open the secrets of the *order* of nature, to do something enormous enough to oblige this order to reveal itself. It is Jehovah, the cruel God of the Old Testament, who is Melville's god, as He is that of Kierkegaard and Kafka; it is Jehovah whom he must get to, who is behind the silent monster in his path.

In my opinion Ahab is descended from Oedipus, Hamlet, and Lear as much as from Faust. He has a furious capacity for interrogation. As is the case with many killers, he would kill his whale, if he could, so as to understand; and it is still that understanding, a moment of Truth, which he pursues at the risk of his own annihilation.

Early in the book, in Chapter XXXVI ("The Quarter-Deck"), we hear this dominant note in Ahab's response to Starbuck's indignation: "Vengeance on a dumb brute! ... that simply smote thee from blindest instinct! Madness! To be enraged with a dumb thing, Captain Ahab, seems blasphemous." But Ahab replies: "All visible objects, man, are but as pasteboard masks. But in each event – in the living act, the undoubted deed – there, some unknown, but still reasoning thing puts forth the mouldings of its features from behind the unreasoning mask. If man will strike, strike through the mask!* How can the prisoner reach outside except by thrusting through the wall? To me, the white whale is that wall, shoved near me. Sometimes I think there's naught beyond...

---

* Who knows whether Melville in this passage was not thinking unconsciously of Hamlet striking through the tapestry? And it is not the king whom Hamlet stabs!

That inscrutable thing is chiefly what I hate." He is Oedipus as he interrogates the enormous severed head of the whale. He is Hamlet: "Speak ... tell us the secret thing that is in thee.... That head ..... has moved amid this world's foundations."

Finally the unanswered question turns to defiance, defiance of the fire of heaven invoked beyond the pale glimmering of St. Elmo's fire. "I know that thy right worship is defiance.... In the midst of the personified impersonal, a personality stands here. [I am] but a point at best ... yet while I earthly live, the queenly personality lives in me, and feels her royal rights come in thy lowest form of love, and I will kneel and kiss thee ...".

But no love is forthcoming, no gratitude for the queenly personality, no consolation for man's metaphysical humiliation. Rejected, the somber hero remains indomitable. And here we have another mystery: alienated from himself and totally alone, watching himself act like a conscious robot, he yet commands. The spiritual force, the *energy* of his Satanism transforms ordinary men into wicked angels, and drags them along with it. Here Ahab becomes a criminal in his total contempt for others, for these men whom he refuses to recognize as people – he who nevertheless demands such a recognition of himself from the universe. His men are mere instruments for him and he dares roar in their face that they are not men, but simply his own arms and legs. Ahab's human impiety damns him without appeal, but it also renders his domination more grandiose and more terrifying.

His sorrow is close to that of Milton's Satan, who, after mounting to the light, looks the Sun straight in the face and says: "To thee I call, But with no friendly voice, and add thy name, O Sun, to tell thee how I hate thy beams...." And Ahab, gazing at the setting sun, says: "This lovely night, it lights not me; all loveliness is anguish to me, since I can ne'er enjoy." Separation from God, from nature, from men, is for him both an ineluctable punishment and a fate which he embraces fiercely.

Furthermore Ahab has succeeded, since the universe has reacted, since the excess of his disorder has unleashed a cosmic disorder, as in a Shakespearian tragedy. We sail with the *Pequod* amid portents, in a universe abandoned by God, occupied by the Devil. It was not for nothing that Ahab broke his sextant. Everything moves backwards: the ship's compass is suddenly found to be pointing the wrong way. Standing at the tiller one night, Ishmael emerges from a strange torpor to find that he too is reversed: he has turned toward the poop and has been guiding the ship backwards.

In these pages, Melville reveals himself as a great visionary.

No author could create such a character and endow him with so much force except at his own expense. Only by bringing into play all the spiritual forces one can find within oneself, all the energy

one can arouse by consuming one's own substance, can a writer hope to create even the imagery of the insurrection of devastation of all human values which take up the last two hundred pages of *Moby Dick*. And Melville paid the price.

PRATIQUE

DE LA PÊCHE

DE LA BALEINE

DANS

LES MERS DU SUD.

Par Jules Lecomte.

RÉDACTEUR EN CHEF DU *Navigateur*.

HAVRE.

J. MORLENT, ÉDITEUR, SOUS LES ARCADES,

HUE, LIBRAIRE, RUE DES DRAPIERS.

1833.

The Ocean

One has only to read Melville's letters to find out how he nursed Ahab's violence and despair, his questioning and his defiance, within his own heart. Yet (and I am not at all sure that this doesn't constitute his chief victory) he was able to keep Ahab at a distance, so that his mystery remains intact. The captain in his madness does not succeed in dragging the book along with him to the depths, even though he manages to jolt it profoundly. And it is because the book is balanced thanks to the writer's perhaps instinctive sense of his craft, which mysteriously tips the scales.

The whaler *Pequod* is much more seriously and profoundly a microcosm than the frigate *Neversink* was; it bears, as Melville is careful to point out, "a delegation of mankind," men of all nations, all races and colors. Queequeg, the fetish-worshipping, pagan harpooner is the eternal comrade who was as necessary to Melville's imagination as woman is to others. In the miserable room at the inn where Ishmael stays before they set sail, he is forced to share his bed with a tattooed savage (those "hieroglyphics" which cover his skin are perhaps a premonition of the whale, of the mystery of the world). He awakes to find Queequeg's arm around him "in the most loving and affectionate manner." He also mentions his "bridegroom clasp," and shows him "hugging a fellow-male in that matrimonial sort of style." This mystic marriage, for it is nothing less than this, of the civilized man and the savage in a particular vision of the Platonic *eros*, reconstitutes man: head and heart, intelligence and sensitive intuition. In any case, it gives the civilized man an idea of what humanity is. "I felt a melting in me. No more my splintered heart and maddened hand were turned against the wolfish world."

It must be noted that while Ahab is distinguished by rigidity and inflexibility, Ishmael allows himself to be converted to man, nature, and God but only after a profound distress: he has now "ceased to stumble against the walls of solitude and derision." And later on, when Queequeg and Ishmael are tied together like two Siamese twins, one on top of the other, or when they weave together the braid that is for Ishmael the image of destiny, their consenting solidarity soothes for a moment the horror Ishmael feels at being so alone, so obscure, so isolated in the world. Queequeg perishes in the universal catastrophe of the boat of hell, but he has saved Ishmael.

In truth, if Ahab-Melville is cursed and condemned, Ishmael-

Melville contained within him the principle of love to which Queequeg gives a human face. When the demons go away, a tender sensuality can allow him to participate in the universe: wonder and ecstasy steal over him. In spite of his resentment toward Goethe and Emerson, he too is capable of feeling himself included in the Whole and he experiences the joy of perfect communion with the material world. As he kneads the whale-sperm he thinks: "After having my hands in it for only a few minutes, my fingers felt like eels, and began, as it were, to serpentine and spiralize ... as I bathed my hands among those soft, gentle globules ... as they richly broke to my fingers, and discharged all their opulence, like fully ripe grapes their wine; as I snuffed up that uncontaminated aroma, – literally and truly, like the smell of spring violets ... while bathing in that bath, I felt divinely free from all ill-will, or petulance, or malice, of any sort whatever."

D. H. Lawrence would say that he was one with nature, that his cruel feeling of separation had found appeasement in the senses. Melville is curiously precise: "I almost began to credit the old Paracelsan superstition that sperm is of rare virtue in allaying the heat of anger...."

This total relaxation, of an at least vaguely sexual sort, is diametrically opposed to the impression of savage sterility and destructive denial which the book as a whole gives us. But almost all communion is included in this one aspect, this one contact. The whale-calves frolicking in the waves are for Ishmael a revelation of the nature of the divine. The white whale itself, against which Ahab has projected all the hatred in the world, is seen very differently by Ishmael: with its vast gleaming hump, the white luminous shadow of its milky forehead, it suggests "A gentle joyousness – mighty mildness of repose in swiftness."

Moby Dick seems to Ishmael like the white bull who carried off Europa and who was none other than Jupiter. Left to his own devices, Ishmael would accept the whale. He is not so wounded that he cannot feel a sense of wonderment when confronted with these *intact* creatures. And thus, like Jonah, he is saved from the abyss which is the whale, the Sea, Death and Nothingness, which is the solitude of hell. He is saved in the way that the sermon at the beginning of the book defines salvation. But his salvation goes unnoticed next to the triumphant damnation of Ahab and his men. Like Milton, (as Blake said of him), Melville finally remains on the side of Satan.

Melville rejected Emerson's conception of the world: he wants no part in a reassuring vision. Yet neither does he want resignation, abnegation of the ego in detachment. Only through a recognition of what man is (Queequeg) and of human brotherhood can one find a meaning in the universe, accept its mystery, feel its splendor, as one follows up that chain of human love. This is a precious dialectic in *Moby Dick*, which must not delude us about the nature of the final argument: terror and solitude.

But the difference between Emerson's security and Melville's anguish is perhaps not exactly there where it seems, or where Melville imagines it to be. Critics have not yet stopped quibbling over the symbolism in *Moby Dick*, nor defining it in more or less psychoanalytical language, depending on the writer. These whimsical approaches are of little importance beside the most essential fact. The Ocean, and the divine and monstrous Beast which is in a way the Ocean's soul, are no doubt accorded the same kind of ontological value that Pascal would have given them: the "Universe," "eternal silence," terror and mystery – we are back in the ancient world. But almost in spite of himself, Melville's language and metaphors shift the question toward us. The real gulf, the real missing link is not that between microcosm and macrocosm, between interior world and universe. It is within us, inside that very interior world itself. The superb fable of *Moby Dick* succeeds in leading us astray, as does Ahab's wound. It is because the fables in *Mardi* never quite managed to exist that one felt that there was nothing more there than man's ego: "To myself, I seem not myself. All I am sure of, is a sort of prickly sensation all over me, which they call life.... By the incomprehensible stranger in me, I say, this body of mine has been rented out scores of times, though always one dark chamber in me is retained by the old mystery."

It seems obvious today that this mystery of that which exists for itself, this impossibility of feeling that one is the master of one's fate, which our humiliated Calvinist discovered, are basically identical with the mystery of being, and Melville is able to pursue them simultaneously. Today we are liable not to realize the importance for Melville's time of a passage such as this: "For as this appalling ocean surrounds the verdant land, so in the soul of man there lies one insular Tahiti, full of peace and joy, but encompassed by all the horrors of the half-known life."

Important, because it attributes this change in direction precisely to the central image of his vision, that of the Ocean. Melville peoples *the deep* with the horrors of the unconscious, of the instinctive creature within us. That which is inside us and which our conscience cannot see nor our will alter is what ultimately constitutes our predestination.

What shows that this is fundamentally Melville's most intimate if not his clearest preoccupation in *Moby Dick* is that it establishes a remarkable continuity between two books which on the surface seem very different: *Moby Dick* and *Pierre*. Conrad's books are likewise in appearance divided into two categories: novels of the sea and novels of the unconscious. And yet there is no essential difference between *The Nigger of the Narcissus* and *Heart of Darkness*.

One of the rare photographs of Melville, taken by R. Dewey

The Kraken

Melville lived *Moby Dick*. Little by little he sank down into terror. He was consumed by fever. At the end óf June, 1851, he emerged, ravaged but still heroic. He writes to Hawthorne: "Shall I send you a fin of the 'Whale' by way of a specimen mouthful? The tail is not yet cooked – tho' the hell-fire in which the whole book is broiled might not unreasonably have cooked it all ere this." Hawthorne had written of *The Scarlet Letter* that it was truly a book burnt with the fires of hell. The two heretic and inveterate puritans thus reveal a striking similarity of attitude toward the way in which their masterpieces were created.

Melville's letters to Hawthorne throughout the autumn of 1851 constantly verge on incoherence, and bear witness to an alarming state of mind, made up of violent impulses and sudden lapses. We can imagine the embarrassment of the prudent Hawthorne, who, like Alfred de Vigny, was not on intimate terms even with himself, when confronted with overflowings of passion which took him directly to task. When the book was published the tension

---

N.B. We have tried to present a selection of Blake's engravings which would give the mood of Melville's works, rather than to illustrate exactly Melville's Christian Prometheianism. In the following pages one will find engravings of Blake illustrating Milton, Dante, and the Book of Job.

Kraken: a kind of fantastic octopus of the Norwegian seas, capable, according to legend, of stopping ships.

scarcely let up, the murmurs and clamorings of the lost soul scarcely died down. Melville replies to Hawthorne who wrote him of his admiration for the book and offered to review it, that he regretted not being at his writing desk when he received Hawthorne's letter – had he been, he would have sat down at once and answered it. "In me divine magnanimities are spontaneous and instantaneous – catch them while you can. I can't write what I felt. But I felt pantheistic then – your heart beat in my ribs and mine in yours, and both in God's. A sense of unspeakable security is in me this moment, on account of your having understood the book."

Security for him who marched all his life in insecurity – how precious and how precarious it must have seemed! Victim of the vertigo of the always fleeting, always uncertain identity, he is no longer the same man who received the letter. After the burst of feeling, the resplendence of a mystic union, of an identity, he finds himself isolated once again. Two days later joy has come flooding back: a joy whose symbolic, allegorical nature may well have been perceptible to his friends. "A sense of unspeakable security is in me this moment, on account of your having understood the book.... Whence come you, Hawthorne? By what right do you drink from my flagon of life? And when I put it to my lips – lo, they are yours and not mine. I feel that the Godhead is broken up like the bread at the Supper, and that we are the pieces. Hence this infinite fraternity of feeling."

Distrust returns immediately: Melville resembles the ailing Rousseau: "You did not care a penny for the book. But, now and then as you read, you understood the pervading thought that impelled the book and that you praised....

"My dear Hawthorne, the atmospheric skepticisms steal into me now, and make me doubtful of my sanity in writing you thus. But, believe me, I am not mad, most noble Festus! So, now, let us add Moby Dick to our blessing, and step from that. Leviathan is not the biggest fish; – I have heard of Krakens.

"This is a long letter, but you are not at all bound to answer it. Possibly, if you do answer it, and direct it to Herman Melville, you will missend it – for the very fingers that now guide this pen are not precisely the same that just took it up and put it on this paper.

"I shall leave the world, I feel, with more satisfaction for having come to know you. Knowing you persuades me more than the Bible of our immortality."

Note in these two successive letters the same phrase about the *unspeakable security* Hawthorne gives him. As though he needed to be reassured by others about himself and about his identity, and as though the next moment that identity slipped through his fingers! One thinks again of Lawrence and of that reassurance Lawrence found in love. It is possible that Melville's life contains secret passions. There is only one love which he reveals to us in such terms as "cup" and "lips" – that love he feels for Hawthorne, a love which mounts out of the depths of despair. Mentally or physically, Melville, after briefly experiencing the consolation one feels on awakening from a nightmare, is sick. . . and *Moby Dick* has made him so.

He hardly had a chance to taste this reassurance when it was withdrawn from him. Doubtless there was no help for it, and one doesn't get rid of the terrors of man's fate merely by evoking them: catharsis has never purged anyone, not the Greek tragedians, nor Shakespeare when he wrote *King Lear*. Far from it! Actually the horrors which Melville believed for a moment he had chased away by bringing them to light were still there: they refused to budge. His phantoms had become monstrously present, were seated comfortably around him in a ring, staring at him. And so he went on with the process he describes in *Pierre:* he dredges up from himself, as from a mine that is dug ever deeper, samples of ore whose appearance is more and more strange and frightening.

But something else intervened to hasten the reappearance of the phantoms. The calm in which Melville imagined he could repose could not result merely from the fact of his having translated his torments into literature; it could at best find support in the public's acceptance of his offering, of his sacrifice, in a comforting harmony with other men and with himself, about himself, by means of his books. If there had been even a ridiculous harmony in the past, he had sometimes denounced it bitterly, sometimes resigned himself to it, to the point of playing Mr. Omoo for Sophia Hawthorne. But since *Mardi* he had gradually hardened. Now the chilly reception given *Moby Dick*, the book in which he had plumbed the limits of his possibilities, was the *failure* he had already foreseen, the failure his pride almost went so far as to proclaim justified, since in this book which he had *written*, he had failed to produce the book *thought* and desired.

Thus once again Melville is alone, like an actor left alone on the stage of a theater by the departing audience. And so he sinks once again into his own desolation. Far from trying to find another formula for equilibrium, as he had done in *Moby Dick*, he now is relentless in cultivating evil and suffering and in proclaiming them.

On December 28, 1851, his friend Sarah Morewood writes: "I hear that he is now engaged in a new work as frequently as not to leave his room till quite dark in the evening – when he for the first time during the whole day partakes of solid food – he must therefore write under a state of morbid excitement which will soon injure his health – I laughed at him somewhat and told him that the recluse life was leading made his city friends think that he was slightly insane – he replied that long ago he had come to the same conclusion himself."

Pierre was apparently written in such a state of mind in a few weeks. The publisher's contract with Harper was as a matter of fact signed as early as February, 1852.

On October 22, 1851, Elizabeth Melville had given birth to a second son. Melville had of course declared himself as the father for the clerk's records, but instead of giving his wife as the mother he had by mistake given the name of his own mother, Mary Gansevoort, born in Albany. Thus it was not a mere slip of the name. In moments of great emotion one can of course make mistakes, one can even persevere in them; but when one reads *Pierre, or the Ambiguities* it is difficult to believe that this accident, occurring when it did, is devoid of significance.

Socially, Pierre is Herman Melville, the descendant of the Gansevoorts. The given name of the general his grandfather is the same. However Pierre is much wealthier than were the Gansevoorts themselves. Melville, who had never had anything, wanted to provide his hero with every advantage so that he might reject them. His father is dead, and Pierre is the only child of a fond, doting mother – another advantage for him to spurn.

Living with his mother and her butler in a luxurious house; lost in a kind of idyll that is more insipid than refined; delicate, scented, feminine, Pierre seems completely ignorant of the realities of life, of men, of suffering, solitude, and evil. He is pure as the virgin snow of his estate, and filled with a generosity of spirit which, having had no opportunity to exercise itself, lacks all discernment. He is in contact with nothing on the outside: he is what Melville calls an *idealist*. Nor does he know his own nature.

One would like to know what Melville had in mind when he began his book by introducing his main character as he does. Did he have a plan or did he begin at random, barging straight ahead with only a notion of confronting a gilded illusion with the harshness of experience? One would like to know, for the vital question here is just when Melville seized upon the concrete images of Pierre's journey toward experience – whether it was at the beginning of the book or later on. Just how did the idea arise in his unconscious of connecting Pierre's revolt with the discovery of a clandestine illegitimate sister whom he will decide to marry in

order to protect her rights – thus rejecting his pale fiancée and even more his overweening mother who is, as a matter of fact, replaced by the sister. The plot curiously parallels Yillah's deliverance by Tadji, that other "idealist," in *Mardi*. But in the case of Pierre it is given a new and fatal cast by the romantic blood relationship, synonymous with natural affinity, exalting equivocal, guilty and chaste raptures. It is the passion that obsessed Shelley and which he bestowed on Laon and Cythna, another pure, married brother-and-sister couple.

The relationship between the son and the mother is, then, full of ambiguities from the beginning. To the mother in her charming widowhood "a reverential and devoted son seemed lover enough"; in her narcissism which might well be a basis for incest, and which is a sign of her immobile, patrician haughtiness, she imagines that she sees "her own graces strangely translated into the opposite sex." To Pierre also these delicate joys seem to be enough: young as he is, he feels the same inclination to shut himself up from the world. The author, who enters completely into his character and speaks his precious, simpering language with a curious complacence, informs us that "much that goes to make up the deliciousness of a wife, already exists in a sister," and that Pierre's young and beautiful mother is a good substitute for a sister. It will be noted how agilely in the "idealistic" context Melville forges ahead, while seeming to ignore the existence of natural instincts. Already the two call each other brother and sister. Pierre slips a ribbon around her neck: "Well, what is to hold it there, Pierre?" she cries, and he answers: "I am going to try and tack it with a kiss, sister."

The mother has taken over the dead father as a part of what she herself represents; and she imposes the worship of his sanctified image which reverts to her. And this is repeated over and over: Pierre's soul is a *sanctuary* with this holy image at its center. The son's attachment to the mother is quite naturally accompanied by an identification with the father which is depicted most precisely in a highly curious scene. Pierre is asking his aunt about a portrait of his father.

"The picture was painted long ago, my child: you were not born then."

"Not born?" cried little Pierre.

"Not born," said his aunt.

"Well, go on, aunt; but don't tell me again that once upon a time I was not little Pierre at all, and yet my father was alive."

No doubt for a dispossessed and hence avid soul – Melville's,

102

if not Pierre's – the horror of having not always existed, rare as it is, may become identified with the more usual horror of having to cease existing some day.

Such as he is, however, Pierre becomes engaged. Or rather, perhaps, he allows himself to be engaged to the pale, blonde, gentle Lucy Tartan. Here again one cannot help but be struck by certain precisions of the sort which one simply does not invent. Lucy sends Pierre to look for an object in her bedroom and he sees the unreal reflection of her bed in the mirror. He is curiously disturbed and depressed by the sight. Shortly thereafter, he meditates on his forthcoming marriage to Lucy and cannot seem to get used to the idea, in spite of the tenderness he feels toward her. "I am of heavy earth and she of airy light.... I am Pluto stealing Proserpine," He feels a stranger to her, and marriage seems unholy to him: it is what Melville calls "the wild anguish of anticipative rapture." Only anguish is certain. It is curious, to say the least, that intentionally or not the author chose to note these inhibitions. He has been married scarcely four years to the gentle, blonde Elizabeth Shaw. To what extent does he identify himself with Pierre?

It is at this point in a Germanic atmosphere heavy with premonitions of trouble ahead that a letter arrives from a dark-haired young girl whom he had glimpsed one day, who had cried out and fainted at the sight of Pierre: she is his sister. And Pierre is face to face with monsters.

He turns first toward his dead father. His father had had an illegitimate daughter. His father, that icon before whom his mother used to kneel, was then a man with a mask. He lied. His face lied. His portrait lied, the portrait that hung in their home. For there was another portrait, an older one, very unlike, and perhaps closer to the man as he really had been.

The theme of the world behind a mask pursues us from book to book. None of them suggests *Hamlet* more strongly than this one. Hamlet was amazed that traitors could smile. Here, "when we would deceive, we smile," thinks Pierre, who feels that he is the heir to "three thousand years of Hamletism." Dante had made him fierce, "and Hamlet had insinuated that there was none to strike." There was no one. That was why Ahab had tried to strike the whale: to reach someone behind the mask. Pierre proclaims: "From all idols, I tear all veils; henceforth I will see the hidden things; and live right out in my own hidden life!" Ahab's decision had been superbly clear, as well as heroic: ranging himself on the

103

side of God's adversary, he would force God to recognize him; through sacrilege he would slip out of the fold in which men are herded together. Pierre (Melville-Pierre) is obscure. The remark of his that would correspond to Ahab's sacrilege is, "I shall lie with my sister!" Even though Melville's thinking has doubtless evolved, nonetheless this is not what Pierre actually says: his challenge remains unuttered. But the sequel, no less tortuous than edifying, to the soul-searching which brings him to this pass would be psychologically more interesting if Melville had been Dostoievsky and had carried his book onto the psychological level, which he does not do and which we are obliged to do for him.

The sin of the father is the passionate, intense dark-haired, young girl who comes out of the night, or, one might almost say, out of a fevered brain. Her past, like Yillah's, is nothing more than a series of strange visions and nameless sufferings, which

form a series of incoherent tableaux around a single theme: solitude, abandonment. Pierre's soul, suddenly invaded and swamped by this sin, this suffering and passion, is given over to chaos, and none of the German Romantics went so far in depicting spiritual disorder. We are close to Ford and Webster. The professed horror, the vision of the destruction of the world and oneself, cloak a violent attraction. Pierre proclaims his repudiation of beauty and joy – but he means the luminous beauty of the light of day. Isabel is a beautiful sin, Luciferian, the color of night.

Behind the living girl is the dead father. Pierre wants to take on the responsibility of both of them, interpose himself between them and the world, where they would find only hostility and condemnation. To give back the girl her rights without dishonoring the father, without having to get the impossible consent of his hypocritical mother, what better solution than to marry her?

Once he has made this decision he feels a somber joy at the thought of it. He has renounced his mother and his fiancée as well as all possibility of happiness; he has taken the path of sacrifice and misfortune. Hamlet has become Christ. This is stated almost explicitly: "In the Enthusiast to Duty, the heaven-begotten Christ is born; and will not own a mortal parent." It is a question of redemption: "Through his father's sin, that father's fair fame now lay at the mercy of the son, and could only be kept inviolate by the son's free sacrifice of all earthly felicity."

So much for the conscious. The unconscious, as Melville sees it, is slightly different: he notices that Pierre's decision to marry his sister for appearances' sake was (perhaps) led up to by his habit of calling his mother "Sister." He does not add that this might have been also facilitated by his treating his mother as a lover. Nonetheless, caught up in the game of ambiguities, ambiguities of fate like those which form the substance of Greek tragedy, ambiguities in human relations, attitudes and behavior, ambiguities of ideas which are never in harmony with reality, ambiguities of words and phrases, Pierre, owing to his virtue and idealism, is heading toward incest. Doubtless he could fall a prey to sexuality only through coercion – remember his anguish at the sight of Lucy's bed. This ideal incest has its counterpart in Faulkner's *The Sound and the Fury*, where Quentin, the passionate idealist, who is a kind of Pierre, takes it into his head to affirm that his sister Caddy is his mistress, as though this fiction were capable of turning all of Caddy's sins toward him, could *reabsorb* and finally annihilate them.

105

Finally, isn't the most important of the things Melville does *not* say, (perhaps because he doesn't dare to), and which would resolve the question of Pierre's defiance, is that there is, in fact, an obscure *wish* to commit incest in his speech and his defiant attitude, and that this constitutes the analogy to the diabolical baptism of the harpoons, the sword piercing the mask? Isn't it just such an implication which gives a meaning to Pierre's wanderings amid the trees and rocks of a wild landscape? At this point he calls upon "the sovereign powers," threatening: "if ye forsake me now" (at this point in the novel, it is quite obvious that they *have* forsaken him) – "farewell to Faith, farewell to Truth, farewell to God; exiled for aye from God and man, I shall declare myself an equal power with both; free to make war on Night and Day, and all thoughts and things of mind and matter, which the upper and nether firmaments do clasp!"

It is not the "If God does not exist, all is permitted" of the *Brothers Karamazov*, which, when one thinks of it, is base and vulgar, and to which one must add: "I can do as I please, I risk nothing that matters to me." It is closer to: "If God exists thus, and if He be other than I imagined, perhaps a God of Evil, let Him show himself, let him approve or condemn the acts which I shall commit in order to oblige him to do so." It is, finally, a hypothesis and an experiment on the part of man, on the part of Melville, behind Pierre, desperate to know the nature of the metaphysical world, just as a physicist might advance hypotheses and conduct experiments in the hope of discovering something about the nature of the physical world.

Melville lacked the necessary courage. And thus Pierre transforms himself even *before* his author developed on paper the course of his acts and decisions from a metaphysician into a lost soul, confused and obscure even to itself. And the physical and metaphysical temptation of incest becomes the psychological obsession of avoiding incest. And the end is uncertain and confused, as in a painting exposed to infra-red light, in which the underpainting shows through the final version.

Pierre makes his decision amid a romantic whirlwind of incoherent and contradictory feelings, which nonetheless take on power from their contact with a violently troubled, violently importuned spirit like that of Macbeth or King Lear. The infernal "powers" of rock and forest surround Pierre as they do characters in Hawthorne or Hardy. *Pierre* bears a certain resemblance to *Jude the Obscure*, even in its author's lack of sufficient detachment in regard to it –

indeed it is not unlike Hardy's work in general – when we remember how Hardy liked to emphasize the fact that his villages and hamlets were a likelier setting for Greek-style tragedy than are large cities, in which the anonymity of individuals and human relations dulls the intensity. Melville writes already: "No dense mob of Ninevah confounds all personal identities in Saddle Meadows." And here, as in *Jude*, decisions are illusory: man is the plaything of the instincts the gods have placed within him and the victim of an idealism which prevents him from discovering what they are, or who he is. He is absurd. In one of his flights of passion, Pierre hugs his sister and at this moment they perceive that their feelings are not those of a brother and sister: "Over the face of Pierre there shot a terrible self-revelation; he imprinted repeated burning kisses upon her." Nothing that he has professed is true. He has sacrificed everything, and his icons have been replaced by idols.

It is at this point that Pierre, feeling the misery of the exile and the misunderstood writer, comes upon the tract of Plotinus Plinlimmon, in which Melville, it has been claimed, was making fun of the transcendentalist movement. Nothing could be more untrue. What Melville found out to his sorrow between *Mardi* and *Pierre* is what he has his hero discover: that absolute morality, that of Christ for instance, is impracticable among men; that it is wise to make the best of relative good; to submit even one's desires and one's need for virtue to this law. Sartre's Goetz traces a more unlikely course from the devil to God, to finish, perhaps, among men. Pierre has gone from the God to the Devil, and the Devil does not let him go.

Pascal had stated simply: "Man is neither angel nor beast, and misfortune rules that he who wishes to become an angel shall become a beast." Pierre, having become a beast while attempting to become an angel, releases hatred and suffering all around him. His mother dies, he kills a man and kills himself with the two women he loves. Before quitting the world he has burned his past, the portrait of his father, and has burned and charred his right hand. It is the symbolic equivalent of Ahab's having been marked by lightning.

The book is dedicated to Mount Graylock or the Mountain of the Titans, and Pierre is a titan pitted against the gods. He has a vision of that mountain in which he dimly sees the effigy of Enceladus thrown from the heights, and he recognizes his own features in that grotesque form, petrified in flight. It is as though Melville had wanted to reinforce the theme of incest in raising it to the cosmic level by means of the myth, and in recalling the story of the old Titan, the grandfather of Enceladus and son of an incestuous union between the earth and the sky. In *White Jacket* there is a curious passage in which Melville establishes at least one connection between incest of the Oedipus kind, as in Sophocles, or Shelley's *The Cenci*, and that which he calls in the undoubted sincerity of his idealism and in spite of his many more or less passionate friendships, "even worse horrors," – in other words, sodomy. We are reminded of Melville's associating these ideas when we see Pierre Glendinning, having cast off his mother and finacée, beg hospitality from his cousin Glendinning Stanly for himself and his "wife" Isabel. (Notice the use of family names which were in use as given names in the Melville and Gansevoort families.) The author evokes at this point the childhood friendship which bound Pierre and his cousin, their daily letters, the ambiguity (still another one!) of a feeling belonging to a period in life – Melville is explicit on this point – when the other sex is not yet the object of a special attraction. Stanly's coolness, the distance separating them, and lies and dissimulation have substituted a new passionate intensity, negative this time, for the old one. Glendinning Stanly insults Pierre Glendinning grossly. But the latter's mother in disinheriting her son has made her nephew her heir, so that it seems that Pierre's identity has been passed on to Glendinning, who now desires Lucy. But Lucy, Pierre's white angel, as Isabel is his black angel, has asked nothing more than to rejoin him, or rather *them* – Isabel and Pierre. It is the conflict raging around Lucy and fresh insults from Stanly who wants to abduct her against her will that cause Pierre to kill him. We can judge of the complexity of Pierre's feelings, and of their fatal nature.

If *Pierre* today looms large in the list of Melville's works, it is because this book which is a failure is well suited to be the story of a failure. Melville discovered, and he expresses it in each of his books, that he who has never known failure cannot become great, that failure is the true proof of glory. Even better, he has discovered it at the very moment when Emerson was forging his philosophy of success. One can imagine how isolated he must have felt!

Between the first part of *Pierre* – the hero's endeavor, experience, action, and revolt – and the second – his passion and annihilation – there is the space of a catastrophe of absolute and total failure; and it is his own failure that Melville without any sign of accepting it is attempting to gauge. Literary failure: when one is left alone with one's work, when the public shuns it, what value can one assign to it? – human failure, failure among men of a heroic conception of life, failure of the idealism in which he plainly feels himself to be deeply involved. Even better, he remains involved. He takes note of the wreck of idealism, and of the morality of the Absolute, but he continues to side with both against man's fate, which refuses to tolerate them. I have mentioned Milton's Satan too often in connection with Ahab not to speak here of Shelley's Prometheus in connection with Pierre; isn't Pierre a titan like the prisoner of the Caucasus? Does he not see in a dream his body cruelly thrown into the depths by Jupiter? In reply to the prosperity of Evil, Pierre proposes Promethean virtue (and not Satanic wickedness), although ambiguity remains even in the last analysis.

A double identification binds the author to his work: on the one hand he has loyally shared in Pierre's madness on the basis of that

"idealism" which he wished to explore in all directions from its sources up to its final consequences; on the other hand he has identified Pierre with his lot as a writer – which results in two novels rather clumsily joined together. While almost all the female intrigue in the book is valuable for its unwitting depiction of the torments of a puritanical soul, the description of the writer's life among "the Apostles" is, in my opinion, the most successful section of the book, though in quite another vein. Here we find the habitual taste, even more profound and bitter than usual, for self-mockery. And what verve he brings to the task! Melville tried – as he had done since *Mardi*, and especially in the latter book and in *Moby Dick* – to lean on his culture. And now, lonelier even than before in all his pride, he realizes that "it was nothing at all to him, what other men had written." He is nothing more than a madman, sitting down at his table made of a board, supported by

110

two barrels in a room from which all human emotion is forbidden. He who in *White Jacket* symbolically opposed the healthy young man who is amputated and massacred to the artificial man who is the surgeon, now becomes in turn the artificial man: "Oh, I hear the leap of the Texan Comanche, as at this moment he goes crashing like a wild deer through the green underbrush; I hear the glorious whoop of savage and untamable health; and then I look in at Pierre. If physical, practical unreason make the savage, which is he? Civilization, Philosophy, Ideal Virtue! behold your victim!"

Pierre was published in July, 1852. The reviews were wretched. Apparently even the Hawthornes had nothing to say about it – they had ceased to be neighbours in spirit as well as in body.

Melville is only thirty-three years old. But in a way he is finished, consumed, like Rimbaud after *A Season in Hell*. Henceforth his irony is silent, masked in its turn; his symbolism becomes fantastic, scornful, mocking. It will be nonetheless significant for seeming less controlled and more ambiguous. He will dispense with all rigid allegory. His language now seems part and parcel of his silence, and gains a new power from it. Melville's therotic was no attempt at communication, a clamor aimed at the Gods, where others, according to their temperament, murmur prayers instead. Now Melville has understood, and in his fellow-man's disdain he perceives that the Absolute ignores his existence. Henceforth in his writing his behavior toward the Absolute will be completely different. Let it keep its masks, its barricades – *he* will never try to pass beyond them. Man's lot in an inhuman universe is to pass from metaphysical rebellion to scornfull dignity – the process begins within man himself, and he notices its archetypes in the world around him. On the personal level, the question of the father is dismissed for the moment, though not settled (in thirty years he will write *Billy Budd*). But it does not involve him alone. All of us are orphans. And now the time for brotherhood has come.

His sensitivity to social injustice, to all the various misfortunes of poor folk and to their enormous courage, his hatred of all cheating and trickery, of all the forces of oppression throughout the world, and even more, his contempt, grimace surreptitiously behind the irony in each tale, each portrait, each fable.

Significantly, the first of these tales and that which closely corresponds to the self-imposed confinement mentioned in letters from his mother and his friends is *Bartleby the Scrivener*. Doubtless we are free to situate the gently-refusing clerk within the author's own personality, like Gregory or the other extraordinary inventions of Kafka. Bartleby says no in his quiet voice as efficiently perhaps as Hawthorne in his voice of thunder. If he must "represent" something precise, perhaps it is the reaffirmation at any price of moral independence against men and the gods. But it has been noted that in each of his stories Melville "plants" a clue to his dominant preoccupation. Here he writes: "At leisure intervals I looked a little into 'Edwards on the Will' and 'Priestley on Necessity'" – so as to conclude, once again, that he had been predestined to *undergo* Bartleby and that he must accept him. This leaves the problem almost intact: what is Bartleby in himself? Perhaps simply that refusal to live which causes him to spend every day in front of a white page because this mission has been assigned to him for all eternity. He *is* Bartleby the scrivener. At any rate Melville had to ask the question, which may be applied also to *Benito Cereno* or to *I and My Chimney*. But, like Kafka, he asks it only because the concrete presents itself with a force which one must try to explain to oneself.

Discouragement and public indifference had the curious effect of relaxing Melville. He gives his imagination free rein, like a man who has renounced great accomplishments. Or rather he lets it flow along, play at will, pounce upon anything that attracts his eye. *The Tartarus of Maids*, for example, allows us to seize his associations of images as they pass, and gives us a glimpse of how he associates images: he goes to get some paper at a factory and remembers suddenly that Locke compared human beings coming into this world to a white pulp. The link is established between procreation and the manufacturing of paper. From now on curious analogies enrich the parallel which there is no further point in masking with the flavor of concreteness, so that procreation may be described *through* the manufacturing of paper. The narrator adapts himself to the situation by becoming a seed-merchant.

And as a matter of fact it matters little whether it is life or literature that sets the chain-reaction of analogies in motion. The humble autobiography of an unfortunate soldier in the American Revolution, Israel Potter, allows our author to use his favorite themes, such as that of the garment which reveals or disguises identity. The sailor doffs by choice the cast-off garment of an aristocrat to don that of a scarecrow even before his definitive degradation. Or the theme of confinement, present since Redburn: Israel Potter is a secret agent hiding in England in the hollow of a thick wall where he imagines he will die of suffocation; then at Benjamin Franklin's house in Paris he is confined in a locked room. The indifference of society toward the insignificant individual, even though he is a hero, inspires Melville's bitterness, and dominates all his leitmotifs.

Likewise the memoirs of Captain Delano furnish the theme of *Benito Cereno*. The theme of masked reality and the ambiguity of appearances has never been closer to the heart of the subject than here. The *San Dominic* has for a figurehead a skeleton masked by a cloth. In the eyes of the honest Delano, the Negro Babo seems meek and docile as a slave, and Benito Cereno seems a languid perverse, capricious, rather contemptible master. In reality, Babo is a diabolical fiend, the head of the mutineers who have seized control of the ship, and his influence over his master stems directly from the threat of his concealed dagger. Yet he hardly exists outside Don Benito: he is a horror which obsesses him, a disease of his soul.

But all this will be revealed only by the documents which accompany the tale, which in itself is a description of the surface of things, smooth, calm and deceitful as the water of a pond. Four years before, Melville would have exerted himself to prove that it was an image of life. The terror in this story proceeds once again from the opaque mystery of appearances and the intentions they conceal. Don Benito Cereno sadly tells Captain Delano: "Your last act was to clutch for a villain, not only an innocent man but the most pitiable of all men."

This period of profound, despairing work ends and fulfills itself in 1856 with *The Confidence Man: His Masquerade*. As usual the setting and characters are symbolic: the action takes place on board the steamer *Fidèle*, a Mississippi steamboat. In no other book does Melville succeed so well with such summary indications at giving an impression of the uproar of a crowd: one thinks of Jonson's *Bartholomew Fair*. A series of characters are introduced; each in turn occupies the foreground, fleeces his victim and then disappears. First a deaf-mute, then a crippled Negro, a stockbroker, a quack doctor, a bereft widower, etc.... But it is always the same man. Yet Melville disdains to make us believe it – he refuses to make the transformations seem credible. We are far beyond realism. The "character" in any case acquires in the course of his appearances an ironic eloquence more and more specious and increasingly significant.

The confidence man is of course a crook. Lack of confidence in him creates misanthropes; lack of confidence in the universe creates atheists. Nothing could be worse.

One hears tell of spurious wines, but "there is . . . a kind of man who, while convinced that on this continent most wines are shams, yet still drinks away at them, accounting wine so fine a thing, that even the sham article is better than none at all."

In opposition to the man who believes or who forces himself to so as to avoid the worst, is the figure of the suspicious man who becomes the guest of the insane-asylum, wherein each inmate is given over to the ravings of solitude. How can one hesitate? Let us have confidence, trust in appearances, especially since we have no means of knowing anything, most of all the hearts of our fellowmen. Panurge hymning the praises of debts as a symbol of human or cosmic solidarity, was a wholesome and reassuring metaphysician compared to this imposter who opposes the logic of distrust to the logic of confidence, and who bases the harmony of the universe and the chances of happiness on a swindle docilely accepted.

The fact that it is a swindler who delivers the theory of belief says a great deal about Melville's spiritual despair around 1855. For, of course, behind the earthly swindle we glimpse the religious one, the concession trade in paradise. And the crooks are in the right, since nothing is safe from attack, everything is masked, and everything in human life and especially the capitalist system whose symbol the crook is, is based on conventions. The masquerade of the subtitle thus takes up this obsessing theme of the universal illusions.

Face to face with the impostor aboard the steamer *Fidèle* is a cynic who offers the antithesis, who mistrusts, sneers, denounces. He is ridiculous, almost odious. He has a wooden leg. "He is missing something," not just his leg but perhaps also a meaning, an inclination to abandon himself to mystery. Melville did not wish there to be a solution. For confidence is not one. The ship's barber has posted a *No Credit* sign. The imposter shames him, makes him sign a *mutual* agreement and take down the sign. Then he has himself shaved and leaves without paying. Thoughtfully, the barber hangs up his sign once more.

Melville is only thirty-seven, but he is as weary as an old man. Tormented by rheumatism, sciatica, neuralgia, and even more by despair, he accepts money for a trip to Europe and leaves on a pilgrimage to the Holy Land.

He sets sail on October 11, 1856. Hardly is he aboard when he notes in his journal, as though his mind had been revolving in the same circle for seven years: "Conversations with the colonel on fixed fate &c."

In Liverpool he sees Hawthorne, now American consul there. The passionate letters (to which however we lack Hawthorne's replies, which Melville destroyed) are only ashes now. Hawthorne in his own journal notes their meeting with a somewhat cold benevolence mingled with pity. "He seemed depressed and aimless," notes Hawthorne's son Julian.

The father, who nonetheless wished to invite the visitor to rest in his home, notes that "he is a person of very gentlemanly instincts in every respect, save that he is a little heterodox in the matter of clean linen." They walk together among the dunes: "Melville, as he always does, began to reason of Providence and futurity, and of everything that lies beyond human ken, and informed me that he had 'pretty much made up his mind to be annihilated'; but still he does not seem to rest in that anticipation; and, I think, will never rest until he gets hold of a definite belief. It is strange how he persists – and has persisted ever since I knew him, and probably long before – in wandering to and fro over these deserts, as dismal and monotonous as the sand hills amid which we were sitting. He can neither believe, nor be comfortable in his unbelief; and he is too honest and courageous not to try to do one or the other. If he were a religious man, he would be one of the most truly religious and reverential; he has a very high and noble nature, and better worth immortality than most of us." He watches him leave with the same gentle, tired curiosity. Melville left behind the bulk of his baggage for the long trip through Europe and the Orient. But after all, hadn't a minimum of baggage always been for Melville a symbol of the human condition, bravely assumed?

Hawthorne and Melville will not meet again. A poem, *Monody*, seems to have been written by Melville after Hawthorne's death:

> To have known him, to have loved him
>   After loneness long;
> And then to be estranged in life,
>   And neither in the wrong;
> And now for death to set his seal –
>   Ease me, a little ease, my song!

When Julian Hawthorne came to see Melville in 1883 to speak with him about his father, he found him restless, nervous, upset at having to reawaken these memories, having burned all his letters and declaring himself convinced that a deep secret in Hawthorne's life was at the root of the mystery in his work. Did he have in mind a similar secret hidden in his own heart?

The Mediterranean jolted his melancholy: with what eagerness Melville looks at a port like Syra, experiences its motion, its masses, its confused perspectives! Nowhere is vitality and the alacrity of his imagination more evident than in this journal which his telegraphic style renders almost comic at first glance. But his vitality constantly runs up against a feeling of frustration, and the renunciation which reality comes to symbolize. Thus he writes of the labyrinthine streets in Constantinople and elsewhere: "No clue. Hopelessly lost."

Throughout his journal the Orient emerges only as a sorrowful allegory: "Went towards the cemeteries of Pera ... saw a woman over a new grave – no grass on it yet. Such abandonment of misery! Called to the dead, put her head down as close to it as possible; as if calling down a hatchway or cellar; besought – 'Why don't you speak to me? My God! Ah, speak – but one word!' – All deaf. – So much for consolation. – This woman and her cries haunt me horribly." Did Melville-Pierre-Hamlet recognize himself and his own cries in this woman? Sometimes, as he watches the spectacle of life in the orient move jerkily past like a marionette show, whose absolute and theatrical strangeness occasionally amuses him, he feels death to be the leitmotif – it is not even, as in Flaubert, an element in "the great synthesis."

Everything strong in the journal is horrible. Horror at the pyramids: "I shudder at the idea of ancient Egyptians. It was in these pyramids that the idea of Jehovah was conceived." Horror in Jerusalem: "Wandering among the tombs – till I began to think myself one of the possessed with devils.... The color of the whole

118

city is gray and looks at you like a cold gray eye in a cold old man. – its strange aspect in the pale olive light of the morning. ..." Horror at the Dead Sea, where he arrives "over a moldy plain ... foam on beach and pebbles like slaver of mad dog – smarting bitter of the water – carried the bitter in my mouth all day – bitterness of life – thought of all bitter things – Bitter is it to be poor & bitter to be reviled." And images of humiliation spring to mind: "Oh bitter are these waters of Death, thought I."

A phrase occurs twice while he is looking at tombs. In Constantinople: ". . . the soldiers of Constantine – sowed in corruption and raised in potatoes." And in Rome: "Tomb with olive trees on it. Sown in corruption, raised in olives." His somber verve can't resist depicting the priest in Jerusalem who sells places in heaven, as though he were selling real estate: "Can't let you have *this* place – taken up. Nor *this*. ..." With morbid delight, he feasts his mind on the spectacle of the ugliness of the commercialization of sacred places. He is disillusioned. But, as Hawthorne noted, he curses his own skepticism: he curses Niebuhr, he curses Strauss, who prevented him from discovering St. John at Patmos: "If they have undeceived any one – no thanks to them." Always it is the integrity of childhood, the happiness of innocence, of confidence, that his nostalgia pursues. We note (in spite of the prevailing mood of this trip which is bitter, skeptical, sometimes cynical) the obstinate nature of his pilgrimage to the sources of religion which has been his intention from the beginning and which he will never lose sight of. One is startled to find so near us a spirit so purely Hebraic. He spends a week at Constantinople, a month in Judaea and Palestine, and three days at Athens, and one would swear that the latter was merely a question of duty with him, that he experienced literally nothing there. He visited no other places in Greece. Ancient Greece does not enter into his mythology.

Melville takes his somber oriental mood with him to Italy. At Posilippo he notes merely: "At Posilippo found not the cessation [of pain] which the name expresses."

In Italy he turns to art. What kind of art? In Rome he buys an engraving of Guido Reni's Beatrice Cenci, which Hawthorne considered the painting in the world with the deepest conception behind it, and which Melville had already described in *Pierre*. He admires the Antinous of the Capitoline Museum, and describes a head of Antinous at the Villa Albani as being "like moss-rose with curls and buds."

Tortured, incestuous beauty, beauty of the feminine man,

119

The corruption of the body. (National Museum, Florence).

fascination of death – such is the impression of Italy that his journal gives. At Florence the wax sculptures of Zummo plunge him in a macabre delectation of death and decay: "No. 2 Vault – heaps – all colors from deep green to buff – all ruins – detached bones – mothers, children, old men – No. 3. rats, vampires, insects, slime and ooze of corruption. – Moralist, this Sicilian .... Horrible humiliation." At Florence on March 26, 1857, "At dinner table accosted by singular young man who speaks 6 or 8 languages. He presented me with a flower, and talked like one to whom the world was delightful." On March 27 he "dined at the Luna with the young Polyglot." But the whole trip passes without his meeting a woman, unless the journal was violently censored. Is it possible, however, that there may have been a grand emotion, a belated and thus all the more overwhelming revelation? It is another secret, which is perhaps hinted at in a poem written afterward which describes an aging and hitherto frigid woman who is suddenly smitten by a young traveling companion, who, in his turn, has eyes only for a young peasant girl whom they meet during their trip.

In 1860, Melville, the former sailor, now becomes a passenger and tourist and sets sail once again around the Americas on the *Meteor*, a boat belonging to his brother Thomas. He soon feels depressed and disappointed, and he cuts short his voyage. Meanwhile his wife had sent Duyckinck a volume of poems prepared by Herman, which Duyckinck forwarded to Scribners who returned them. With dignity, Elizabeth writes that she is sure of her husband's poems, that she will wait for an occasion to publish them. It will be the war poems, the *Battle-Pieces*, which will be published first, in 1866. Four months later, Melville is sworn in as customs inspector of the port of New York. Forgotten by the public for years, he will no longer write anything but poems to please himself. The long poem *Clarel*, published with difficulty in 1876 thanks to Elizabeth's devotion, is the spiritual autobiography of a Christian soul trying to find itself in the modern world. Vine, the character who is bored by long developments of theory and who always remains reserved, is doubtless Hawthorne. Rolfe, the former sailor who remembers an island where the natives once acclaimed him as a god descended from heaven, is obviously in large part an em-

This copy is specially presented to my wife, without whose assistance in manifold ways I hardly know how I could have got the book (under the circumstances) into shape, and finally through the press. Herman Melville

bodiment of Melville. A nostalgia for the spiritual unity of the Middle Ages penetrates this so very un-American poem, which opposes both the materialism and the idealism of the nineteenth century. "Let us listen to the heart," says this son of Calvinism now, as he denounces protestant intellectualism and seems to be harking to the siren's songs of Cardinal Newman. A difficult lesson! One could not say that his personality had suddenly become imbued with a gentle radiance. Melville was a morose, perhaps cruel father, unloved by his children. His eldest son Malcolm was found dead in his bedroom one morning at the age of eighteen. He had committed suicide. The second never amounted to anything. One of his daughters always recalled her childhood with aversion. Death was all around Melville; he read Schopenhauer and became interested in the gloomiest poet in English literature, James Thomson, author of *The City of Dreadful Night*.

In 1889 he received Balzac's *Correspondance* as a gift. How close he must have felt to that embittered, sad, heroic giant, who had sacrificed his life to his art and his thought! He meditates on the letter to Madame Hanska, dated October 1, 1836: "Doubtless you did not know of the profound grief that is in my soul, nor what somber courage accompanies my second great defeat, undergone in the midstream of my life....

"For a whole month I have risen at midnight and gone to bed at six, eaten only what is necessary to remain alive.... Sometimes I lose my sense of equilibrium. Even in bed it seems that my head is falling from left to right, and when I get up I feel carried away by an enormous weight inside my head. *I can understand how the absolute ascetism of Pascal and his immense labours, brought him to the pass that he saw constantly an abyss on both sides of him, and was obliged to have two chairs on each side of the one in which he sat.*"

The italics are Melville's. He recognized and nodded to the abyss in passing.

Elizabeth Shaw Melville in 1885.

Melville's
BILLY BUDD

EDITED BY
F. BARRON FREEMAN

THE COMPLETE TEXT OF THE NOVEL
AND OF THE UNPUBLISHED SHORT STORY

Published by Harvard University Press

God Bless Captain Vere

And yet it is in these circumstances that he began to write *Billy Budd* in 1888. He had finished it just before his death in 1891. Disdained, the book remained in manuscript until 1924.

In 1842, when he was roaming in Tahiti, Lieutenant Guert Gansevoort, his cousin, voyaging aboard the brig *Somers* had discovered or imagined that he had discovered a plot to take over the ship. He had denounced it to the commanding officer, determined to have a young midshipman and two petty-officers condemned, and they were hung from the main yard. The part played by one of his relatives in this drama no doubt contributed toward arousing the spirit of justice and humanity in the author of *White Jacket* and toward implanting the subject in his mind. The Commander, seized by a nameless remorse, begged one of the condemned men, Small, to bid him good-by. Small had replied, "I did not know that you would bid a poor bugger like me good-by, sir." And he had added, "God bless that flag!"

Billy Budd is the story of a foretopman unjustly accused by Claggart, the master-at-arms, of having fomented a mutiny. It is set in 1797, at the time of a famous series of mutinies in the English navy. Claggart is the last of Melville's damned, diabolical demons. Like the first, Jackson, he mingles knavery and baseness with his diabolicism. He hates Billy Budd as Lucifer hated Adam, for his very purity, for his angelic beauty and the quasi-femininity which gives it transparency. This brief book is centered round the mystery of natural depravity and destructive hate, around that "nostalgia for purity" which, in Claggart, Melville associates with hate.

Billy Budd appears in the presence of his accuser before the commander, Captain Vere. In the violence of the emotion which overwhelms him and paralyzes his tongue, so that he is unable to defend himself, Billy Budd strikes the master-at-arms who falls dead. Billy Budd is a foundling; when asked who his father was, he replies, "God knows, Sir." Yet in reality, vague hints seem to point to the fact that, unknown to either of them, Captain Vere is perhaps his father. At any rate the latter feels strange tenderness for this young seaman, who seems to radiate some ineffable glory, even after he has struck down his miserable foe. But his duty as master of the ship wins out over this feeling and over his understanding of human values. He is not free. Nor are the officers charged with the court martial free. They must condemn Billy Budd. Billy has discovered a father who understands and loves him. But the very circumstances that have given rise to this love force this father to demand his death by hanging. It is the mystery of Abraham's sacrifice, but no messenger comes to stay his hand or sever the knot: the sacrifice must be consummated. The death of Billy Budd, foretopman, is like an ascension to glory; the mainyard takes on the mystical aspect of a cross and afterwards the men preserve the wood. Before he dies, Billy Budd says "God bless Captain Vere!"

Thus Melville at the very moment his death has arrived, many years after *Mardi*, in the harbor of peace and grace, on the Christian island of Serenia: in the person of Billy Budd, he has accepted the mystery of death and suffering, the obvious horror and injustice of our lot, everything, down to the silence that turns a man to stone when he wants to speak. The limpidity of the story, the purity that radiates from its hero, that calmed melody which is heard here as in the gilded reconciliations of Shakespeare's last plays, all seems to indicate that he had accepted them for himself as well.

It seems now as if the very meaning of the quest for a father, begun so long ago, had changed for him. "When shall we be done growing?" he had asked Hawthorne in 1851. Now he has finished growing. The serenity of detachment has created the figure of Captain Vere who is double, heart and law, and who separates

Billy Budd

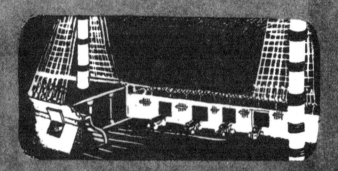

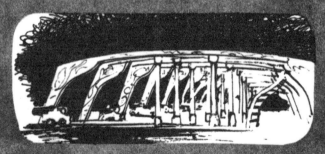

Benjamin Britten

heart from law like a British law court. The law must be applied so that the existing order of the world (the ship) will not slide toward chaos. No one is free with regard to the law – neither he who applies it, nor he who bows to it. The father is not there to be kind nor the son to be happy, but one and the other for the sacred bond that joins them. Certainly a world other than this ship-world is conceivable, in which we would be subject to the law. Billy Budd has been taken from the merchant vessel *Rights-of-Man* and transferred aboard the *Indomitable*. But the *Rights-of-Man*, before Billy arrived with his radiant, masculine gentleness, was nothing but quarreling and disorder; this is perhaps the image of a world without law. Transferred into the world of law, this gentleness was not wasted. It filled men's hearts and imaginations.

We are far from this world today, and Kafka, who seems to connect us with it, shows us the width of the gulf, in which the ultimate consequences of the law are experienced only with horror, so that Billy Budd's sacrifices might correspond to the horrible murder of K. by the two emissaries. "But the hands of one of the two partners already held K. by the throat, while the other planted the knife in his heart and turned it twice. As his sight faded, K. saw them still, both of them, cheek to cheek, gazing down at him, waiting for the final act. Like a dog! he said. It was as though he had wanted the shame of the thing to survive him."

On April, 19, 1891, Melville in his fluid, slanting handwriting, transcribed Billy Budd's last poem:

> But me, they'll lash me in a hammock, drop me deep.
> Fathoms down, fathoms down, how I'll dream fast asleep.
> I feel it stealing now. Sentry, are you there?
> Just ease these darbies at the wrist.
> And roll me over fair.
> I am sleepy, and the oozy weeds about me twist.

End of Book

April 19, 1891

Fathoms down, down, how I'll dream.

Fast asleep.

I feel it stealing now. Sentry, are you there?

Just ease this iron at the wrist,

and roll me over fair,

I am drowsy, and the oozy weeds

about me twist.

— // —

End of Book   April 19 1891

The last page of the manuscript of Billy Budd.

Melville died on September 28. A once popular author, said the newspapers. He was rediscovered on the occasion of the hundredth anniversary of his birth. *Billy Budd*, which had seemed to slumber among the oozy weeds, was published for the first time in 1924. Melville's work was henceforth complete for men to study. They have reclassified it as he would have wished, with regard to that frenzied exploration to which he devoted himself beginning with *Mardi*, and in which *Typee* and *Omoo* count for little. They have confronted in turn the Leviathan and the Kraken; they have re-edited and translated *Pierre*, which in 1852 had remained before the public just long enough to scandalize its readers and caused them to call Melville a madman. The mystery of the man has scarcely been explored, but he is before us approximately as he would have wished to be. Each of us can find in himself enough elements of Melville's personality to have some inkling of the whole, however personal may be that conception.

MARDI

HERMAN MELVILLE

Texts

MARDI

Mardi is the book whose depths obliged Hawthorne "to swim for his life." An ambiguous and perhaps slightly malicious compliment, which recognizes the profundity and hints at flight.

Surrounding the allegorical paraphernalia is the obstinate presence of the sea. It is the sea, with its abysses and its immensity, truly felt for the first time in this third novel, which permits Melville to pass directly from the concrete particular to the universal, from reality to symbol.

Chapter CLXV

THEY ROUND THE STORMY CAPE OF CAPES

Long leagues, for weary days, we voyaged along that coast, till we came to regions where we multiplied our mantles.

The sky grew overcast. Each night, black storm-clouds swept

the wintry sea; and like Sahara caravans, which leave their sandy wakes – so, thick and fleet, slanted the scud behind. Through all this rack and mist, ten thousand foam-flaked dromedary-humps arose.

Deep among those panting, moaning fugitives, the three canoes raced on.

And now, the air grew nipping cold. The clouds shed off their fleeces; a snow-hillock, each canoe; our beards, white-frosted.

And so, as seated in our shrouds, we sailed in among great mountain passes of ice-isles; from icy ledges scaring shivering seals, and white bears, musical with icicles, jingling from their shaggy ermine.

Far and near, in towering ridges, stretched the glassy Andes; with their own frost, shuddering through all their domes and pinnacles. Ice-splinters rattled down the cliffs, and seethed into the sea.

Broad away, in amphitheaters undermined by currents, whole cities of ice-towers, in crashes, toward one center, fell. – In their earthquakes, Lisbon and Lima never saw the like. Churned and broken in the boiling tide, they swept off amain; – over and over rolling; like porpoises to vessels tranced in calms, bringing down the gale.

At last, rounding an antlered headland, that seemed a moose at bay – ere long, we launched upon blue lake-like waters, serene as Windermere, or Horicon. Thus, from the boisterous storms of youth, we glide upon senility.

But as we northward voyaged, another aspect wore the sea.

In far-off, endless vistas, colonnades of water-spouts were seen: all heaven's dome upholding on their shafts: and bright forms gliding up and down within. So at Luz, in his strange vision, Jacob saw the angels...

Chapter CLXVIII

CONCENTRIC, INWARD, WITH MARDI'S REEF, THEY LEAVE THEIR WAKE AROUND THE WORLD

... Over balmy waves, still westward sailing! From dawn till eve, the bright, bright days sped on, chased by the gloomy nights; and, in glory dying, lent their luster to the starry skies. So, long the radiant dolphins fly before the sable sharks; but seized, and torn in flames – die, burning: – their last splendor left, in sparkling scales that float along the sea....

WHITE JACKET

The following selection is one of the numerous passages, descriptive or otherwise, which Melville inserted in **White Jacket** *and which he could have inserted almost anywhere. The teratological collection of the ship's surgeon could very well be Melville's collection: most significant here is the description of the monstrous, accursed head of a woman; it is easy to see in it traces of the painful doctrine of pre-destination which Melville had imbibed with the milk of his Calvinist education. Yet notice the cast he gives it. Evil and innate sin become the cruellest form of misfortune, and Calvinist reprobation stirs an intense, fraternal pity within him: Man's revolt against his plight is unformulated here but fleetingly visible. As with Baudelaire, evil and misfortune are part of our dignity, and our only liberty consists in our assuming them.*

The Ship's Museum.

Chief among these was a cast, often to be met with in the Anatomical Museums of Europe, and no doubt an unexaggerated copy of a genuine original; it was the head of an elderly woman, with an aspect singularly gentle and meek, but at the same time wonderfully expressive of a gnawing sorrow, never to be relieved. You would almost have thought it the face of some abbess, for some unspeakable crime voluntarily sequestered from human society, and leading a life of agonised penitence without hope, so marvellously sad and tearfully pitiable was this head. But when you first beheld it, no such emotions ever crossed your mind. All your eyes and all your horrified soul were fast fascinated and frozen by the sight of a hideous, crumpled horn, like that of a ram, downward growing out from the forehead, and partly shadowing the face; but as you gazed, the freezing fascination of its horribleness gradually waned, and then your whole heart burst with sorrow, as you contemplated those aged features, ashy pale and wan. The horn seemed the mark of a curse for some mysterious sin, conceived and committed before the spirit had entered the flesh. Yet that sin seemed something imposed, and not voluntarily sought; some sin growing out of the heartless necessities of the predestination of things; some sin under which the sinner sank in sinless woe.

The following episode is something other than a bravura passage: it is a striking intuition about the human personality, the co-existence

*of the life-wish and the death-wish, and the way in which the con-
science makes itself felt at the uttermost limits of both.*

*Feeling the revolting touch of the fish, a foreign presence, at the
moment when one is about to let oneself slide into the ecstatic union
with nothingness, defines superbly the regain of consciousness and
will, or resurrection from these waters of forgetfulness. In reality,
Melville had thrown his white jacket into the water – a symbolic
suicide, like Mrs. Dalloway's when she throws her shilling into the
Serpentine.*

Chapter XCII

THE LAST OF THE JACKET

. . . Having reeved the line through all the inferior block, I went
out with it to the end of the weather-top-gallant yard-arm, and was
in the act of leaning over and passing it through the suspended
jewel-block there, when the ship gave a plunge in the sudden swells
of the calm sea, and pitching me still further over the yard, threw
the heavy skirts of my jacket right over my head, completely muffl-
ing me. Somehow I thought it was the sail that had flapped, and
under that impression, threw up my hands to drag it from my head,
relying upon the sail itself to support me meanwhile. Just then the
ship gave another sudden jerk, and, head foremost, I pitched from
the yard. I knew where I was, from the rush of the air by my ears,
but all else was a nightmare. A bloody film was before my eyes,
through which, ghost-like, passed and repassed my father, mother,
and sisters. An unutterable nausea oppressed me; I was conscious
of gasping; there seemed no breath in my body. It was over one
hundred feet that I fell – down, down, with lungs collapsed as in
death. Ten thousand pounds of shot seemed tied to my head, as
the irresistible law of gravitation dragged me, head foremost and
straight as a die, toward the infallible centre of this terraqueous
globe. All I had seen, and read, and heard, and all I had thought
and felt in my life, seemed intensified in one fixed idea in my soul.
But dense as this idea was, it was made up of atoms. Having fallen
from the projecting yard-arm end, I was conscious of a collected
satisfaction in feeling that I should not be dashed on the deck, but
would sink into the speechless profound of the sea.

With the bloody, blind film before my eyes, there was a still
stranger hum in my head, as if a hornet were there; and I thought
to myself, Great God! this is Death! Yet these thoughts were

unmixed with alarm. Like frostwork that flashes and shifts its scared hues in the sun, all my braided, blended emotions were in themselves icy cold and calm.

So protracted did my fall seem, that I can even now recall the feeling of wondering how much longer it would be, ere all was over and I struck. Time seemed to stand still, and all the worlds seemed poised on their poles, as I fell, soul-becalmed, through the eddying whirl and swirl of the maelstrom air.

At first, as I have said, I must have been precipitated head foremost; but I was conscious, at length, of a swift, flinging motion of my limbs, which involuntarily threw themselves out, so that at last I must have fallen in a heap. This is more likely, from the circumstance, that when I struck the sea, I felt as if some one had smote me slantingly across the shoulder and along part of my right side.

As I gushed into the sea, a thunder-boom sounded in my ear; my soul seemed flying from my mouth. The feeling of death flooded over me with the billows. The blow from the sea must have turned me, so that I sank almost feet foremost through a soft, seething, foamy lull. Some current seemed hurrying me away; in a trance I yielded and sank deeper down with a glide. Purple and pathless was the deep calm now around me, flecked by summer lightnings in an azure afar. The horrible nausea was gone; the bloody, blind film turned a pale green; I wondered whether I was yet dead, or still dying. But of a sudden some fashionless form brushed my side – some inert, soiled fish of the sea; the thrill of being alive again tingled in my nerves, and the strong shunning of death shocked me through.

For one instant an agonising revulsion came over me as I found myself utterly sinking. Next moment the force of my fall was expended; and there I hung, vibrating in mid-deep. What wild sounds then rang in my ear! One was a soft moaning, as of low waves on the beach; the other wild and heartlessly jubilant, as of the sea in the height of a tempest. Oh soul! thou then heardest life and death: as he who stands upon the Corinthian shore hears both the Ionian and the Aegean waves. The life-and-death poise soon passed; and then I found myself slowly ascending, and caught a dim glimmering of light.

Quicker and quicker I mounted; till at last I bounded up like a buoy, and my whole head was bathed in the blessed air.

I had fallen in a line with the main-mast; I now found myself nearly abreast of the mizen-mast, the frigate slowly gliding by like a black world in the water. Her vast hull loomed out of the night, showing hundreds of seamen in the hammock nettings, some tossing over ropes, others madly flinging overboard the hammocks; but I was too far out from them immediately to reach what they threw. I essayed to swim toward the ship; but instantly I was conscious of a feeling like being pinioned in a feather bed, and moving my hands, felt my jacket puffed out above my tight girdle with water. I strove to tear it off; but it was looped together here and there, and the strings were not then to be sundered by hand. I whipped out my knife, that was tucked at my belt, and ripped my jacket straight up and down, as if I were ripping open myself. With a violent struggle, I then burst out of it, and was free. Heavily soaked, it slowly sank before my eyes.

Sink! sink! oh shroud! thought I; sink forever! accursed jacket that thou art!

"See that white shark!" cried a horrified voice from the taffrail; "he'll have that man down his hatchway! Quick! the *grains!* the *grains!*"

The next instant that barbed bunch of harpoons pierced through and through the unfortunate jacket, and swiftly sped with it out of sight.

Chapter LI

THE SPIRIT-SPOUT

Days, weeks passed, and under easy sail, the ivory Pequod had slowly swept across four several cruising-grounds; that off the Azores; off the Cape de Verdes; on the Plate (so called), being off the mouth of the Rio de la Plata; and the Carrol Ground, an unstaked, watery locality, southerly from St. Helena.

It was while gliding through these latter waters that one serene and moonlight night, when all the waves rolled by like scrolls of silver; and, by their soft, suffusing seethings, made what seemed a silvery silence, not a solitude: on such a silent night a silvery jet was seen far in advance of the white bubbles at the bow. Lit up by the moon, it looked celestial; seemed some plumed and glittering god uprising from the sea. Fedallah first descried this jet. For of these moonlight nights, it was his wont to mount to the main-mast head, and stand a look-out there, with the same precision as if it had been day. And yet, though herds of whales were seen by night, not one whaleman in a hundred would venture a lowering for them. You may think with what emotions, then, the seamen beheld this old Oriental perched aloft at such unusual hours; his turban and the moon, companions in one sky. But when, after spending his uniform interval there for several successive nights without uttering a single sound; when, after all this silence, his unearthly voice was heard announcing that silvery, moon-lit jet, every reclining mariner started to his feet as if some winged spirit had lighted in the rigging, and hailed the mortal crew. "There she blows!" Had the trump of judgment blown, they could not have quivered more; yet still they felt no terror; rather pleasure. For though it was a most unwonted hour, yet so impressive was the cry, and so deliriously exciting, that almost every soul on board instinctively desired a lowering.

Walking the deck with quick, side-lunging strides, Ahab commanded the t'gallant sails and royals to be set, and every stunsail spread. The best man in the ship must take the helm. Then, with every mast-head manned, the piled-up craft rolled down before the wind. The strange, upheaving, lifting tendency of the taffrail breeze filling the hollows of so many sails, made the buoyant, hovering deck to feel like air beneath the feet; while still she rushed along, as if two antagonistic influences were struggling in her – one to mount direct to heaven, the other to drive yawingly to some horizontal goal. And had you watched Ahab's face that night, you would have thought that in him also two different things were warring. While his one live leg made lively echoes along the deck, every stroke of his dead limb sounded like a coffin-tap. On life and death this old man walked. But though the ship so swiftly sped, and though from every eye, like arrows, the eager glances shot, yet the silvery jet was no more seen that night. Every sailor swore he saw it once, but not a second time.

This midnight-spout had almost grown a forgotten thing, when, some days after, lo! at the same silent hour, it was again announced: again it was descried by all; but upon making sail to overtake it, once more it disappeared as if it had never been. And so it served us night after night, till no one heeded it but to wonder at it. Mysteriously jetted into the clear moonlight, or starlight, as the case might be; disappearing again for one whole day, or two days, or three; and somehow seeming at every distinct repetition to be advancing still further and further in our van, this solitary jet seemed for ever alluring us on.

Nor with the immemorial superstition of their race, and in accordance with the preternaturalness, as it seemed, which in many things invested the Pequod, were there wanting some of the seamen who swore that whenever and wherever descried, at however remote times, or in however far apart latitudes and longitudes, that unnearable spout was cast by one self-same whale; and that whale, Moby Dick. For a time, there reigned, too, a sense of peculiar dread at this flitting apparition, as if it were treacherously beckoning us on and on, in order that the monster might turn round upon us, and rend us at last in the remotest and most savage seas.

These temporary apprehensions, so vague but so awful, derived a wondrous potency from the contrasting serenity of the weather, in which, beneath all its blue blandness, some thought there lurked a devilish charm, as for days and days we voyaged along, through seas so wearily, lonesomely mild, that all space, in repugnance to our vengeful errand, seemed vacating itself of life before our urn-like prow.

But, at last, when turning to the eastward, the Cape winds began howling around us, and we rose and fell upon the long, troubled seas that are there; when the ivory-tusked Pequod sharply bowed to the blast, and gored the dark waves in her madness, till, like

138

showers of silver chips, the foam-flakes flew over her bulwarks; then all this desolate vacuity of life went away, but gave place to sights more dismal than before.

Close to our bows, strange forms in the water darted hither and thither before us; while thick in our rear flew the inscrutable sea-ravens. And every morning, perched on our stays, rows of these birds were seen; and spite of our hootings, for a long time obstinately clung to the hemp, as though they deemed our ship some drifting, uninhabited craft; a thing appointed to desolation, and therefore fit roosting-place for their homeless selves. And heaved and heaved, still unrestingly heaved the black sea, as if its vast tides were a conscience; and the great mundane soul were in anguish and remorse for the long sin and suffering it had bred.

Cape of Good Hope, do they call ye? Rather Cape Tormentoto, as called of yore; for long allured by the perfidious silences that before had attended us, we found ourselves launched into this tormented sea, where guilty beings transformed into those fowls and these fish, seemed condemned to swim on everlastingly without any haven in store, or beat that black air without any horizon. But calm, snow-white, and unvarying; still directing its fountain of feathers to the sky; still beckoning us on from before, the solitary jet would at times be descried.

During all this blackness of the elements, Ahab, though assuming for the time the almost continual command of the drenched and dangerous deck, manifested the gloomiest reserve; and more seldom than ever addressed his mates. In tempestuous times like these, after everything above and aloft has been secured, nothing more can be done but passively to await the issue of the gale. Then Captain and crew become practical fatalists. So, with his ivory leg inserted into its accustomed hole, and with one hand firmly grasping a shroud, Ahab for hours and hours would stand gazing dead to windward, while an occasional squall of sleet or snow would all but congeal his very eyelashes together. Meantime, the crew driven from the forward part of the ship by the perilous seas that burstingly broke over its bows, stood in a line along the bulwarks in the waist; and the better to guard against the leaping waves, each man had slipped himself into a sort of bowline secured to the rail, in which he swung as in a loosened belt. Few or no words were spoken; and the silent ship, as if manned by painted sailors in wax, day after day tore on through all the swift madness and gladness of the demoniac waves. By night the same muteness of humanity before the shrieks of the ocean prevailed; still in silence the men swung in the bowlines; still wordless Ahab stood up to the blast. Even when wearied nature seemed demanding repose he would not seek that repose in his hammock. Never could Starbuck forget the old man's aspect, when one night going down into the cabin to mark how the barometer stood, he saw him with closed eyes sitting straight in his floor-screwed chair; the rain and half-melted sleet of the storm from which he had some time before emerged, still slowly dripping from the unremoved hat and coat. On the table beside him lay unrolled one of those charts of tides and currents which have previously been spoken of. His lantern swung from his tightly clenched hand. Though the body was erect, the head was thrown back so that the closed eyes were pointed towards the needle of the tell-tale that swung from a beam in the ceiling.

Terrible old man! thought Starbuck with a shudder, sleeping in this gale, still thou steadfastly eyest thy purpose.

All sail being set, [Ahab] now cast loose the life-line, reserved for swaying him to the main royal-mast head; and in a few moments they were hoisting him thither, when, while but two thirds of the way aloft, and while peering ahead through the horizontal vacancy between the main-top-sail and top-gallant-sail, he raised a gull-like cry in the air, "There she blows! – there she blows! A hump like a snow-hill! It is Moby Dick!"

Fired by the cry which seemed simultaneously taken up by the three look-outs, the men on deck rushed to the rigging to behold the famous whale they had so long been pursuing. Ahab had now gained his final perch, some feet above the other look-outs, Tashtego standing just beneath him on the cap of the top-gallant-mast, so that the Indian's head was almost on a level with Ahab's heel. From this height the whale was now seen some mile or so ahead, at every roll of the sea revealing his high sparkling hump, and regularly jetting his silent spout into the air. To the credulous mariners it seemed the same silent spout they had so long ago beheld in the moonlit Atlantic and Indian Oceans.

"And did none of ye see it before?" cried Ahab, hailing the perched men all around him.

"I saw him almost that same instant, sir, that Captain Ahab did, and I cried out," said Tashtego.

"Not the same instant; not the same – no, the doubloon is mine, Fate reserved the doubloon for me. *I* only; none of ye could have raised the White Whale first. There she blows! there she blows! – there she blows! There again! – there again!" he cried, in long-drawn, lingering, methodic tones, attuned to the gradual prolongings of the whale's visible jets. "He's going to sound! In stunsails! Down top-gallant-sails! Stand by three boats. Mr. Starbuck, remember, stay on board, and keep the ship. Helm there! Luff, luff a point! So; steady, man, steady! There go flukes! No, no; only black water! All ready the boats there? Stand by, stand by! Lower me, Mr. Starbuck; lower, lower, – quick, quicker!" and he slid through the air to the deck.

"He is heading straight to leeward, sir," cried Stubb, "right away from us; cannot have seen the ship yet."

"Be dumb, man! Stand by the braces! Hard down the helm! – brace up! Shiver her! – shiver her! – So; well that ! Boats, boats!"

Soon all the boats but Starbuck's were dropped; all the boat-sails set – all the paddles plying; with rippling swiftness, shooting to leeward; and Ahab heading the onset. A pale, death-glimmer lit up Fedallah's sunken eyes; a hideous motion gnawed his mouth.

Like noiseless nautilus shells, their light prows sped through the sea; but only slowly they neared the foe. As they neared him, the ocean grew still more smooth; seemed drawing a carpet over its waves; seemed a noon-meadow, so serenely it spread. At length the breathless hunter came so nigh his seemingly unsuspecting prey, that his entire dazzling hump was distinctly visible, sliding along the sea as if an isolated thing, and continually set in a revolving ring of finest, fleecy, greenish foam. He saw the vast, involved wrinkles of the slightly projecting head beyond. Before it, far out on the soft Turkish-rugged waters, went the glistening white shadow from his broad, milky forehead, a musical rippling playfully accompanying the shade; and behind, the blue waters interchangeably flowed over into the moving valley of his steady wake; and on either hand bright bubbles arose and danced by his side. But these were broken again by the light toes of hundreds of gay fowls softly feathering the sea, alternate with their fitful flight; and like to some flag-staff rising from the painted hull of an argosy, the tall but shattered pole of a recent lance projected from the white whale's back; and at intervals one of the cloud of soft-toed fowls hovering, and to and fro skimming like a canopy over the fish, silently perched and rocked on this pole, the long tail feathers streaming like pennons.

A gentle joyousness – a mighty mildness of repose in swiftness, invested the gliding whale. Not the white bull Jupiter swimming away with ravished Europa clinging to his graceful horns; his lovely, leering eyes sideways intent upon the maid; with smooth bewitching fleetness, rippling straight for the nuptial bower in Crete; not Jove, not that great majesty Supreme! did surpass the glorified White Whale as he so divinely swam.

On each soft side – coincident with the parted swell, that but once leaving him, then flowed so wide away – on each bright side, the whale shed off enticings. No wonder there had been some among the hunters who namelessly transported and allured by all this serenity, had ventured to assail it; but had fatally found that quietude but the vesture of tornadoes. Yet calm, enticing calm, oh, whale! thou glidest on, to all who for the first time eye thee, no matter how many in that same way thou may'st have bejuggled and destroyed before.

And thus, through the serene tranquillities of the tropical sea, among waves whose hand-clappings were suspended by exceeding rapture, Moby Dick moved on, still withholding from sight the full terrors of his submerged trunk, entirely hiding the wrenched hideousness of his jaw. But soon the fore part of him slowly rose from the water; for an instant his whole marbleized body formed a high arch, like Virginia's Natural Bridge, and warningly waving his bannered flukes in the air, the grand god revealed himself, sounded, and went out of sight. Hoveringly halting, and dipping on the wing, the white sea-fowls longingly lingered over the agitated pool that he left.

With oars apeak, and paddles down, the sheets of their sails adrift, the three boats now stilly floated, awaiting Moby Dick's reappearance.

"An hour," said Ahab, standing rooted in his boat's stern; and he gazed beyond the whale's place, towards the dim blue spaces and wide wooing vacancies to leeward. It was only an instant; for again his eyes seemed whirling round in his head as he swept the watery circle. The breeze now freshened; the sea began to swell.

"The birds! – the birds!" cried Tashtego.

In long Indian file, as when herons take wing, the white birds were now all flying towards Ahab's boat; and when within a few yards began fluttering over the water there, wheeling round and round, with joyous, expectant cries. Their vision was keener than man's; Ahab could discover no sign in the sea. But suddenly as he peered down and down into its depths, he profoundly saw a white living spot no bigger than a white weasel, with wonderful celerity uprising, and magnifying as it rose, till it turned, and then there were plainly revealed two long crooked rows of white, glistening teeth, floating up from the undiscoverable bottom. It was Moby Dick's open mouth and scrolled jaw; his vast, shadowed bulk still half blending with the blue of the sea. The glittering mouth yawned beneath the boat like an open-doored marble tomb; and giving one sidelong sweep with his steering oar, Ahab whirled the craft aside from this tremendous apparition. Then, calling upon Fedallah to change places with him, went forward to the bows, and seizing Perth's harpoon, commanded his crew to grasp their oars and stand by to stern.

Now, by reason of this timely spinning round the boat upon its axis, its bow, by anticipation, was made to face the whale's head while yet under water. But as if perceiving this stratagem, Moby Dick, with that malicious intelligence ascribed to him, sidelingly transplanted himself, as it were, in an instant, shooting his pleated head lengthwise beneath the boat.

144

Through and through; through every plank and each rib, it thrilled for an instant, the whale obliquely lying on his back, in the manner of a biting shark, slowly and feelingly taking its bows full within his mouth, so that the long, narrow, scrolled lower jaw curled high up into the open air, and one of the teeth caught in a row-lock. The bluish pearl-white of the inside of the jaw was within six inches of Ahab's head, and reached higher than that. In this attitude the White Whale now shook the slight cedar as a mildly cruel cat her mouse. With unastonished eyes Fedallah gazed, and crossed his arms; but the tiger-yellow crew were tumbling over each other's heads to gain the uttermost stern.

And now, while both elastic gunwales were springing in and out, as the whale dallied with the doomed craft in this devilish way; and from his body being submerged beneath the boat, he could not be darted at from the bows, for the bows were almost inside of him, as it were; and while the other boats involuntarily paused, as before a quick crisis impossible to withstand, then it was that monomaniac Ahab, furious with this tantalizing vicinity of his foe, which placed him all alive and helpless in the very jaws he hated; frenzied with all this, he seized the long bone with his naked hands, and wildly strove to wrench it from its gripe. As now he thus vainly strove, the jaw slipped from him; the frail gunwales bent in, collapsed, and snapped, as both jaws, like an enormous shears, sliding further aft, bit the craft completely in twain, and locked themselves fast again in the sea, midway between the two floating wrecks. These floated aside, the broken ends drooping, the crew at the stern-wreck clinging to the gunwales, and striving to hold fast to the oars to lash them across.

At that preluding moment, ere the boat was yet snapped, Ahab, the first to perceive the whale's intent, by the crafty upraising of his head, a movement that loosed his hold for the time; at that moment his hand had made one final effort to push the boat out of the bite. But only slipping further into the whale's mouth, and tilting over sideways as it slipped, the boat had shaken off his hold on the jaw; spilled him out of it, as he leaned to the push; and so he fell flat-faced upon the sea.

Ripplingly withdrawing from his prey, Moby Dick now lay at a little distance, vertically thrusting his oblong white head up and down in the billows; and at the same time slowly revolving his whole spindled body; so that when his vast wrinkled forehead rose – some twenty or more feet out of the water – the now rising swells, with all their confluent waves, dazzlingly broke against it;

vindictively tossing their shivered spray still higher into the air.*
So, in a gale, the but half baffled Channel billows only recoil from
the base of the Eddystone, triumphantly to overleap its summit
with their scud.

But soon resuming his horizontal attitude, Moby Dick swam
swiftly round and round the wrecked crew; sideways churning the
water in his vengeful wake, as if lashing himself up to still another
and more deadly assault. The sight of the splintered boat seemed
to madden him, as the blood of grapes and mulberries cast before

---

* This motion is peculiar to the sperm whale. It receives its designation
(pitchpoling) from its being likened to that preliminary up-and-down poise
of the whale-lance, in the exercise called pitchpoling, previously described.
By this motion the whale must best and most comprehensively view whatever objects may be encircling him.

From amateur's drawing to motion picture: the whale's attack.

Antiochus's elephants in the book of Maccabees. Meanwhile Ahab half smothered in the foam of the whale's insolent tail, and too much of a cripple to swim, – though he could still keep afloat, even in the heart of such a whirlpool as that; helpless Ahab's head was seen, like a tossed bubble which the least chance shock might burst. From the boat's fragmentary stern, Fedallah incuriously and mildly eyed him; the clinging crew, at the other drifting end, could not succor him; more than enough was it for them to look to themselves. For so revolvingly appalling was the White Whale's aspect, and so planetarily swift the ever-contracting circles he made, that he seemed horizontally swooping upon them. And though the other boats, unharmed, still hovered hard by; still they dared not pull into the eddy to strike, lest that should be the signal for the instant destruction of the jeopardized castaways, Ahab and all; nor in that case could they themselves hope to escape. With straining eyes, then, they remained on the outer edge of the direful zone, whose centre had now become the old man's head.

Meantime, from the beginning all this had been descried from the ship's mast-heads; and squaring her yards, she had borne down upon the scene; and was now so nigh, that Ahab in the water hailed her; – "Sail on the" – but that moment a breaking sea dashed on him from Moby Dick, and whelmed him for the time. But struggling out of it again, and chancing to rise on a towering crest, he shouted, – "Sail on the whale! – Drive him off!"

The Pequod's prows were pointed; and breaking up the charmed circle, she effectually parted the white whale from his victim. As he sullenly swam off, the boats flew to the rescue.

Dragged into Stubb's boat with blood-shot, blinded eyes, the white brine caking in his wrinkles; the long tension of Ahab's bodily strength did crack, and helplessly he yielded to his body's doom for a time, lying all crushed in the bottom of Stubb's boat, like one trodden under foot of herds of elephants. Far inland, nameless wails came from him, as desolate sounds from out ravines.

But this intensity of his physical prostration did but so much the more abbreviate it. In an instant's compass, great hearts sometimes condense to one deep pang, the sum total of those shallow pains kindly diffused through feebler men's whole lives. And so, such hearts, though summary in each one suffering; still, if the gods decree it, in their life-time aggregate a whole age of woe, wholly made up of instantaneous intensities; for even in their pointless centres, those noble natures contain the entire circumferences of inferior souls.

"The harpoon," said Ahab, half way rising, and draggingly leaning on one bended arm – "is it safe?"

The whale-hunter's spare time.

THE ENCANTADAS

It is said that Milton's walks in the fields around Naples came to his mind when he had to describe hell. Melville had recognized it when he had made a long cruise to the Galapagos Islands, in the autumn of 1841. It is that hell that he invokes in the "sketches" of 1854.

The Isles at Large

Take five-and-twenty heaps of cinders dumped here and there in an outside city lot; imagine some of them magnified into mountains, and the vacant lot the sea; and you will have a fit idea of the general aspect of the Encantadas, or Enchanted Isles. A group rather of extinct volcanoes than of isles; looking much as the world at large might, after a penal conflagration.

It is to be doubted whether any spot of earth can, in desolateness, furnish a parallel to this group. Abandoned cemeteries of long ago, old cities by piecemeal tumbling to their ruin, these are melancholy enough; but, like all else which has but once been associated with humanity they still awaken in us some thoughts of sympathy, however sad. Hence, even the Dead Sea, along with whatever other emotions it may at times inspire, does not fail to touch in the pilgrim some of his less unpleasurable feelings.

And as for solitariness; the great forests of the north, the expanses of unnavigated waters, the Greenland ice-fields, are the profoundest of solitudes to a human observer; still the magic of their changeable tides and seasons mitigates their terror; because, though unvisited by men, those forests are visited by the May; the remotest seas reflect familiar stars even as Lake Erie does; and in the clear air of a fine Polar day, the irradiated, azure ice shows beautifully as malachite.

But the special curse, as one may call it, of the Encantadas, that which exalts them in desolation above Idumea and the Pole, is that to them change never comes; neither the change of seasons nor of sorrows. Cut by the Equator, they know not autumn and they know not spring; while already reduced to the lees of fire, ruin itself can work little more upon them. The showers refresh the deserts, but in these isles, rain never falls. Like split Syrian gourds, left withering in the sun, they are cracked by an everlasting drought beneath a torrid sky. "Have mercy upon me," the wailing spirit of

151

the Encantadas seems to cry, "and send Lazarus that he may dip
the tip of his finger in water and cool my tongue, for I am tormented in this flame."

Another feature in these isles is their emphatic uninhabit-
ableness. It is deemed a fit type of all-forsaken overthrow, that
the jackal should den in the wastes of weedy Babylon; but the
Encantadas refuse to harbour even the outcasts of the beasts.
Man and wolf alike disown them. Little but reptile life is here
found: – tortoises, lizards, immense spiders, snakes, and the
strangest anomaly of outlandish Nature, the *aguano*. No voice, no
low, no howl is heard; the chief sound of life here is a hiss.

On most of the isles where vegetation is found at all, it is more
ungrateful than the blankness of Aracama. Tangled thickets of
wiry bushes, without fruit and without a name, springing up
among deep fissures of calcined rock, and treacherously masking
them; or a parched growth of distorted cactus trees.

In many places the coast is rock-bound, or more properly,
clinker-bound; tumbled masses of blackish or greenish stuff like
the dross of an iron-furnace, forming dark clefts and caves here
and there, into which a ceaseless sea pours a fury of foam; over-
hanging them with a swirl of grey, haggard mist, amidst which
sail screaming flights of unearthly birds heightening the dismal din.
However calm the sea without, there is no rest for these swells and
those rocks, they lash and are lashed, even when the outer ocean
is most at peace with itself. On the oppressive, clouded days such
as are peculiar to this part of the watery Equator, the dark vitrified
masses, many of which raise themselves among white whirlpools
and breakers in detached and perilous places off the shore, present
a most Plutonian sight. In no world but a fallen one could such
lands exist.

Those parts of the strand free from the marks of fire stretch
away in wide level beaches of multitudinous dead shells, with here
and there decayed bits of sugar-cane, bamboos, and cocoanuts,
washed upon this other and darker world from the charming palm
isles to the westward and southward; all the way from Paradise to
Tartarus; while mixed with the relics of distant beauty you will
sometimes see fragments of charred wood and mouldering ribs of
wrecks. Neither will any one be surprised at meeting these last,
after observing the conflicting currents which eddy throughout
nearly all the wide channels of the entire group. The capriciousness
of the tides of air sympathizes with those of the sea. Nowhere is
the wind so light, baffling, and every way unreliable, and so given

to perplexing calms, as at the Encantadas. Nigh a month has been spent by a ship going from one isle to another, though but thirty miles between; for owing to the force of the current, the boats employed to tow barely suffice to keep the craft from sweeping upon the cliffs, but do nothing toward accelerating her voyage. Sometimes it is impossible for a vessel from afar to fetch up with the group itself, unless large allowances for prospective lee-way have been made ere its coming in sight. And yet, at other times, there is a mysterious indraft, which irresistibly draws a passing vessel among the isles, though not bound to them.

True, at one period, as to some extent at the present day, large fleets of whalemen cruised for Spermaceti upon what some seamen call the Enchanted Ground. But this, as in due place will be described, was off the great outer isle of Albemarle, away from the intricacies of the smaller isles, where there is plenty of sea-room; and hence, to that vicinity, the above remarks do not altogether apply; though even there the current runs at times with singular force, shifting, too, with as singular a caprice. Indeed, there are seasons when currents quite unaccountable prevail for a great distance round about the total group, and are so strong and irregular as to change a vessel's course against the helm, though sailing at the rate of four or five miles the hour. The difference in the reckonings of navigators produced by these causes, along with the light and variable winds, long nourished a persuasion that there existed two distinct clusters of isles in the parallel of the Encantadas, about a hundred leagues apart. Such was the idea of their earlier visitors, the Buccaneers; and as late as 1750, the charts of that part of the Pacific accorded with the strange delusion. And this apparent fleetingness and unreality of the locality of the isles was most probably one reason for the Spaniards calling them the Encantada, or Enchanted Group.

But not uninfluenced by their character, as they now confessedly exist, the modern voyager will be inclined to fancy that the bestowal of this name might have in part originated in that air of spellbound desertness which so significantly invests the isles. Nothing can better suggest the aspect of once living things malignly crumbled from ruddiness into ashes. Apples of Sodom, after touching, seem these isles.

However wavering their place may seem by reason of the currents, they themselves, at least to one upon the shore, appear invariably the same: fixed, cast, glued into the very body of cadaverous death.

Nor would the appellation, enchanted, seem misapplied in still another sense. For concerning the peculiar reptile inhabitant of these wilds – whose presence gives the group its second Spanish name, Gallipagos – concerning the tortoises found here, most mariners have long cherished a superstition, not more frightful than grotesque. They earnestly believe that all wrecked sea-officers, more especially commodores and captains, are at death (and in some cases, before death) transformed into tortoises; thenceforth dwelling upon these hot aridities, sole solitary Lords of Asphaltum.

Doubtless so quaintly dolorous a thought was originally in-

spired by the woe-begone landscape itself, but more particularly, perhaps, by the tortoises. For apart from their strictly physical features, there is something strangely self-condemned in the appearance of these creatures. Lasting sorrow and penal hopelessness are in no animal form so suppliantly expressed as in theirs; while the thought of their wonderful longevity does not fail to enhance the impression.

Nor even at the risk of meriting the charge of absurdly believing in enchantments, can I restrain the admission that sometimes, even now, when leaving the crowded city to wander out July and August among the Adirondack Mountains, far from the influences

The cemetery of Atooi.

of towns and proportionally nigh to the mysterious ones of Nature; when at such times I sit me down in the mossy head of some deep-wooded gorge, surrounded by prostrate trunks of blasted pines, and recall, as in a dream, my other and far-distant rovings in the baked heart of the charmed isles; and remember the sudden glimpses of dusky shells, and long languid necks protruded from the leafless thickets; and again have beheld the vitreous inland rocks worn down and grooved into deep ruts by ages and ages of the slow draggings of tortoises in quest of pools of scanty water; I can hardly resist the feeling that in my time I have indeed slept upon evilly enchanted ground.

Nay, such is the vividness of my memory, or the magic of my fancy, that I know not whether I am not the occasional victim of optical delusion concerning the Gallipagos. For often in scenes of social merriment, and especially at revels held by candle light in old-fashioned mansions – when the shadows are thrown into the further recesses of an angular and spacious room, making them put on a look of haunted undergrowth of lonely woods – I have drawn the attention of my comrades by my fixed gaze and sudden change of air, as I have seemed to see, slowly emerging from those imagined solitudes, and heavily crawling along the floor, the ghost of a gigantic tortoise, with "Memento..." burning in live letters upon his back.

View of Broadway around 1850.

BARTLEBY THE SCRIVENER

I wanted to give the main part, if not all this amazing story.
I have reduced it, arbitrarily no doubt, to a symbolic drama with
two characters, by eliminating certain secondary characters – those
of the other clerks in the office who appear in passages whose
humor is in a possibly less personal vein, not dissimilar from that
of Dickens or even Mark Twain. I suspect that, as happens in
Melville, they are there to give the reader a little distraction.
Unless I am mistaken, I have preserved what counted most for
Melville in Bartleby.

. . . In answer to my advertisement, a motionless young man one
morning stood upon my office threshold, the door being open, for
it was summer. I can see that figure now – pallidly neat, pitiably
respectable, incurably forlorn! It was Bartleby.

After a few words touching his qualifications, I engaged him,
glad to have among my corps of copyists a man of so singularly
sedate an aspect, which I thought might operate beneficially upon
the flighty temper of Turkey, and the fiery one of Nippers.

I should have stated before that ground glass folding doors
divided my premises into two parts, one of which was occupied by
my scriveners, the other by myself. According to my humour I
threw open these doors, or closed them. I resolved to assign
Bartleby a corner by the folding-doors, but on my side of them, so
as to have this quiet man within easy call, in case any trifling thing
was to be done. I placed his desk close up to a small side-window
in that part of the room, a window which originally had afforded
a lateral view of certain grimy back-yards and bricks, but which,
owing to subsequent erections, commanded at present no view at
all, though it gave some light. Within three feet of the panes was a
wall, and the light came down from far above, between two lofty
buildings, as from a very small opening in a dome. Still further to
a satisfactory arrangement, I procured a high green folding screen,
which might entirely isolate Bartleby from my sight, though
not remove him from my voice. And thus, in a manner, privacy
and society were conjoined.

At first Bartleby did an extraordinary quantity of writing. As if
long famishing for something to copy, he seemed to gorge himself
on my documents. There was no pause for digestion. He ran a
day and night line, copying by sun-light and by candle-light. I
should have been quite delighted with his application, had he been

cheerfully industrious. But he wrote on silently, palely, mechanically.

It is, of course, an indispensable part of a scrivener's business to verify the accuracy of his copy, word by word. Where there are two or more scriveners in an office, they assist each other in this examination, one reading from the copy, the other holding the original. It is a very dull, wearisome, and lethargic affair. I can readily imagine that to some sanguine temperaments it would be altogether intolerable. For example, I cannot credit that the mettlesome poet Byron would have contentedly sat down with Bartleby to examine a law document of, say five hundred pages, closely written in a crimpy hand.

Now and then, in the haste of business, it had been my habit to assist in comparing some brief document myself, calling Turkey or Nippers for this purpose. One object I had in placing Bartleby so handy to me behind the screen, was to avail myself of his services on such trivial occasions. It was on the third day, I think, of his being with me, and before any necessity had arisen for having his own writing examined, that, being much hurried to complete a small affair I had in hand, I abruptly called to Bartleby. In my haste and natural expectancy of instant compliance, I sat with my head bent over the original on my desk, and my right hand sideways, and somewhat nervously extended with the copy, so that immediately upon emerging from his retreat, Bartleby might snatch it and proceed to business without the least delay.

In this very attitude did I sit when I called to him, rapidly stating what it was I wanted him to do – namely, to examine a small paper with me. Imagine my surprise, nay, my consternation, when without moving from his privacy, Bartleby in a singularly mild, firm voice, replied, "I would prefer not to."

I sat awhile in perfect silence, rallying my stunned faculties. Immediately it occurred to me that my ears had deceived me, or Bartleby had entirely misunderstood my meaning. I repeated my request in the clearest tone I could assume. But in quite as clear a one came the previous reply, "I would prefer not to."

"Prefer not to," echoed I, rising in high excitement, and crossing the room with a stride. "What do you mean? Are you moonstruck? I want you to help me compare this sheet here – take it," and I thrust it toward him.

"I would prefer not to," said he.

I looked at him steadfastly. His face was leanly composed; his grey eye dimly calm. Not a wrinkle of agitation rippled him.

Had there been the least uneasiness, anger, impatience or impertinence in his manner; in other words, had there been anything ordinarily human about him; doubtless I should have violently dismissed him from the premises. But as it was, I should have as soon thought of turning my pale plaster-of-paris bust of Cicero out of doors. I stood gazing at him awhile, as he went on with his own writing, and then reseated myself at my desk. This is very strange, thought I. What had one best do? But my business hurried me. I concluded to forget the matter for the present, reserving it for my future leisure. So calling Nippers from the other room, the paper was speedily examined.

A few days after this, Bartleby concluded four lengthy documents, being quadruplicates of a week's testimony taken before me in my High Court of Chancery. It became necessary to examine them. It was an important suit, and great accuracy was imperative. Having all things arranged, I called Turkey, Nippers and Ginger Nut from the next room, meaning to place the four copies in the hands of my four clerks, while I should read from the original. Accordingly Turkey, Nippers and Ginger Nut had taken their seats in a row, each with his document in hand, when I called to Bartleby to join this interesting group.

"Bartleby! quick, I am waiting."

I heard a slow scrape of his chair legs on the uncarpeted floor, and soon he appeared standing at the entrance of his hermitage.

"What is wanted?" said he mildly.

"The copies, the copies," said I hurriedly. "We are going to examine them. There" – and I held toward him the fourth quadruplicate.

"I would prefer not to," he said, and gently disappeared behind the screen.

For a few moments I was turned into a pillar of salt, standing at the head of my seated column of clerks. Recovering myself, I advanced toward the screen, and demanded the reason for such extraordinary conduct.

"*Why* do you refuse?"

"I would prefer not to."

With any other man I should have flown outright into a dreadful passion, scorned all further words, and thrust him ignominiously from my presence. But there was something about Bartleby that not only strangely disarmed me, but in a wonderful manner touched and disconcerted me. I began to reason with him.

"These are your own copies we are about to examine. It is

labour saving to you, because one examination will answer for your four papers. It is common usage. Every copyist is bound to help examine his copy. Is it not so? Will you not speak? Answer!"

"I prefer not to," he replied in a flute-like tone. It seemed to me that while I had been addressing him, he carefully revolved every statement that I made; fully comprehended the meaning; could not gainsay the irresistible conclusion; but, at the same time, some paramount consideration prevailed with him to reply as he did.

"You are decided, then, not to comply with my request – a

request made according to common usage and common sense?"

He briefly gave me to understand that on that point my judgment was sound. Yes: his decision was irreversible.

It is not seldom the case that when a man is browbeaten in some unprecedented and violently unreasonable way, he begins to stagger in his own plainest faith. He begins, as it were, vaguely to surmise that, wonderful as it may be, all the justice and all the reason are on the other side. Accordingly, if any disinterested persons are present, he turns to them for some reinforcement for his own faltering mind.

"Turkey," said I, "what do you think of this? Am I not right?"

"With submission, sir," said Turkey, with his blandest tone, "I think that you are."

"Nippers," said I, "what do *you* think of it?"

"I think I should kick him out of the office."

(The reader of nice perceptions will here perceive that, it being morning, Turkey's answer is couched in polite and tranquil terms but Nippers's reply in ill-tempered ones. Or, to repeat a previous sentence, Nippers's ugly mood was on duty, and Turkey's off.)

"Ginger Nut," said I, willing to enlist the smallest suffrage in my behalf, "what do *you* think of it?"

"I think, sir, he's a little *luny*," replied Ginger Nut, with a grin.

"You hear what they say," said I, turning towards the screen, "come forth and do your duty."

But he vouchsafed no reply. I pondered a moment in sore perplexity. But once more business hurried me. I determined again to postpone the consideration of this dilemma to my future leisure. With a little trouble we made out to examine the papers without Bartleby, though at every page or two, Turkey deferentially dropped his opinion that this proceeding was quite out of the common; while Nippers, twitching in his chair with a dyspeptic nervousness, ground out between his set teeth occasional hissing maledictions against the stubborn oaf behind the screen. And for his (Nippers's) part, this was the first and the last time he would do another man's business without pay.

Meanwhile Bartleby sat in his hermitage, oblivious to everything but his own peculiar business there.

Some days passed, the scrivener being employed upon another lengthy work. His late remarkable conduct led me to regard his ways narrowly. I observed that he never went to dinner; indeed that he never went any where. As yet I had never of my personal knowledge known him to be outside of my office. He was a perpetual sentry in the corner. At about eleven o'clock though, in the morning, I noticed that Ginger Nut would advance towards the opening in Bartleby's screen, as if silently beckoned thither by a gesture invisible to me where I sat. The boy would then leave the office jingling a few pence, and reappear with a handful of ginger-nuts which he delivered in the hermitage, receiving two of the cakes for his trouble.

He lives, then, on ginger-nuts, thought I; never eats a dinner, properly speaking; he must be a vegetarian then; but no; he never eats even vegetables, he eats nothing but ginger-nuts. My mind then ran on in reveries concerning the probable effects upon the human constitution of living entirely on ginger-nuts. Ginger-nuts are so called because they contain ginger as one of their peculiar constituents, and the final flavouring one. Now what was ginger? A hot, spicy thing. Was Bartleby hot and spicy? Not at all. Ginger, then, had no effect upon Bartleby. Probably he preferred it should have none.

Nothing so aggravates an earnest person as a passive resistance. If the individual so resisted be of a not inhumane temper, and the resisting one perfectly harmless in his passivity; then, in the better moods of the former, he will endeavour charitably to construe to his imagination what proves impossible to be solved by his judgment. Even so, for the most part, I regarded Bartleby and his ways. Poor fellow! thought I, he means no mischief; it is plain he intends no insolence; his aspect sufficiently evinces that his eccentricities are involuntary. He is useful to me. I can get along with him. If I turn him away, the chances are he will fall in with some less indulgent employer, and then he will be rudely treated, and perhaps driven forth miserably to starve. Yes. Here I can cheaply purchase a delicious self-approval. To befriend Bartleby; to humour him in his strange wilfulness, will cost me little or nothing, while I lay up in my soul what will eventually prove a sweet morsel for my conscience. But this mood was not invariable with me. The passiveness of Bartleby sometimes irritated me. I felt strangely goaded on to encounter him in new opposition, to elicit some angry spark from him answerable to my own. But indeed I might as well have essayed to strike fire with my knuckles against a bit of Windsor soap. But one afternoon the evil impulse in me mastered me, and the following little scene ensued:

"Bartleby," said I, "when those papers are all copied, I will compare them with you."

"I would prefer not to."

"How? Surely you do not mean to persist in that mulish vagary?"
No answer...

...I closed the doors, and again advanced towards Bartleby. I felt additional incentives tempting me to my fate. I burned to be rebelled against again. I remembered that Bartleby never left the office.

"Bartleby," said I, "Ginger Nut is away; just step round to the Post Office, won't you? (it was but a three minutes' walk), and see if there is anything for me."

"I would prefer not to."

"You *will* not?"

"I *prefer* not."

I staggered to my desk, and sat there in a deep study. My blind inveteracy returned. Was there any other thing in which I could procure myself to be ignominiously repulsed by this lean, penniless wight? – my hired clerk? What added thing is there, perfectly reasonable, that he will be sure to refuse to do?

"Bartleby!"

No answer.

"Bartleby," in a louder tone.

No answer.

"Bartleby," I roared.

Like a very ghost, agreeably to the laws of magical invocation, at the third summons, he appeared at the entrance of his hermitage.

"Go to the next room, and tell Nippers to come to me."

"I prefer not to," he respectfully and slowly said, and mildly disappeared.

"Very good, Bartleby," said I, in a quiet sort of serenely severe self-possessed tone, intimating the unalterable purpose of some terrible retribution very close at hand. At the moment I half intended something of the kind. But upon the whole, as it was drawing towards my dinner-hour, I thought it best to put on my hat and walk home for the day, suffering much from perplexity and distress of mind.

Shall I acknowledge it? The conclusion of this whole business was, that it soon became a fixed fact of my chambers, that a pale young scrivener, by the name of Bartleby, had a desk there; that he copied for me at the usual rate of four cents a folio (one hundred words); but he was permanently exempt from examining the work done by him, that duty being transferred to Turkey and Nippers, out of compliment doubtless to their superior acuteness; moreover, said Bartleby was never on any account to be despatched on the most trivial errand of any sort; and that even if entreated to take upon him such a matter, it was generally understood that he would prefer not to – in other words, that he would refuse point-blank.

As days passed on, I became considerably reconciled to Bartleby. His steadiness, his freedom from all dissipation, his incessant industry (except when he chose to throw himself into a standing revery behind his screen), his great stillness, his unalterableness of demeanour under all circumstances, made him a valuable acquisition. One prime thing was this, – *he was always there;* – first in the morning, continually through the day, and the last at night. I had a singular confidence in his honesty. I felt my most precious papers perfectly safe in his hands. Sometimes to be sure I could not, for the very soul of me, avoid falling into sudden spasmodic passions with him. For it was exceeding difficult to bear in mind all the time those strange peculiarities, privileges, and unheard of exemptions, forming the tacit stipulations on Bartleby's part under which he remained in my office. Now and then, in the eagerness of despatching pressing business, I would inadvertently summon Bartleby, in a short, rapid tone, to put his finger, say, on the incipient tie of a bit of red tape with which I was about compressing some papers. Of course, from behind the screen the usual answer, "I prefer not to," was sure to come; and then, how could a human creature with the common infirmities of our nature, refrain from bitterly exclaiming upon such perverseness – such unreasonableness. However, every added repulse of this sort which I received only tended to lessen the probability of my repeating the inadvertence.

Here it must be said, that according to the custom of most legal gentlemen occupying chambers in densely-populated law buildings there were several keys to my door. One was kept by a woman residing in the attic, which person weekly scrubbed and daily swept and dusted my apartments. Another was kept by Turkey for convenience sake. The third I sometimes carried in my own pocket. The fourth I knew not who had.

Now, one Sunday morning I happened to go to Trinity Church, to hear a celebrated preacher, and finding myself rather early on the ground, I thought I would walk round to my chambers for awhile. Luckily I had my key with me; but upon applying it to the lock, I found it resisted by something inserted from the inside. Quite surprised, I called out; when to my consternation a key was turned from within; and thrusting his lean visage at me, and holding the door ajar, the apparition of Bartleby appeared, in his

Birds Eye View

TRINITY CHURCH, NEW-YORK.

shirt sleeves, and otherwise in a strangely tattered dishabille, saying quietly that he was sorry, but he was deeply engaged just then, and – preferred not admitting me at present. In a brief word or two, he moreover added, that perhaps I had better walk round the block two or three times, and by that time he would probably have concluded his affairs.

Now, the utterly unsurmised appearance of Bartleby, tenanting my law-chambers of a Sunday morning, with his cadaverously gentlemanly *nonchalance*, yet withal firm and self-possessed, had such a strange effect upon me, that incontinently I slunk away from my own door, and did as desired. But not without sundry twinges of impotent rebellion against the mild effrontery of this unaccountable scrivener. Indeed, it was his wonderful mildness chiefly, which not only disarmed me, but unmanned me, as it were. For I consider that one, for the time, is in a way unmanned when he tranquilly permits his hired clerk to dictate to him, and order him away from his own premises. Furthermore, I was full of uneasiness as to what Bartleby could possibly be doing in my office in his shirt sleeves, and in an otherwise dismantled condition of a Sunday morning. Was anything amiss going on? Nay, that was out of the question. It was not to be thought of for a moment that Bartleby was an immoral person. But what could he be doing there – copying? Nay again, whatever might be his eccentricities, Bartleby was an eminently decorous person. He would be the last man to sit down to his desk in any state approaching to nudity. Besides, it was Sunday; and there was something about Bartleby that forbade the supposition that he would by any secular occupation violate the proprieties of the day.

Nevertheless, my mind was not pacified; and full of a restless curiosity, at last I returned to the door. Without hindrance I inserted my key, opened it, and entered. Bartleby was not to be seen. I looked round anxiously, peeped behind his screen; but it was very plain that he was gone. Upon more closely examining the place, I surmised that for an indefinite period Bartleby must have ate, dressed, and slept in my office, and that too without plate, mirror, or bed. The cushioned seat of a rickety old sofa in one corner bore the faint impress of a lean, reclining form. Rolled away under his desk, I found a blanket; under the empty grate, a blacking box and brush; on a chair, a tin basin, with soap and a ragged towel; in a newspaper a few crumbs of ginger-nuts and a morsel of cheese. Yes, thought I, it is evident enough that Bartleby has been making his home here, keeping bachelor's hall all by himself. Immediately then the thought came sweeping across me, What miserable friendlessness and loneliness are here revealed! His poverty is great; but his solitude, how horrible! Think of it. Of a Sunday, Wall Street is deserted as Petra; and every night of every day it is an emptiness. This building too, which of week-days hums with industry and life, at nightfall echoes with sheer vacancy, and all through Sunday is forlorn. And here Bartleby makes his home; sole spectator of a solitude which he has seen all populous – a sort of innocent and transformed Marius brooding among the ruins of Carthage!

For the first time in my life a feeling of overpowering stinging melancholy seized me. Before, I had never experienced aught but a not-unpleasing sadness. The bond of a common humanity now drew me irresistibly to gloom. A fraternal melancholy! For both I and Bartleby were sons of Adam. I remembered the bright silks and sparkling faces I had seen that day, in gala trim, swan-like sailing down the Mississippi of Broadway; and I contrasted them with the pallid copyist, and thought to myself, Ah, happiness courts the light, so we deem the world is gay; but misery hides aloof, so we deem that misery there is none. These sad fancyings – chimeras, doubtless, of a sick and silly brain – led on to other and more special thoughts, concerning the eccentricities of Bartleby. Presentiments of strange discoveries hovered round me. The scrivener's pale form appeared to me laid out, among uncaring strangers, in its shivering winding sheet.

Suddenly I was attracted by Bartleby's closed desk, the key in open sight left in the lock.

I mean no mischief, seek the gratification of no heartless curiosity, thought I; besides, the desk is mine, and its contents, too, so I will make bold to look within. Everything was methodically arranged, the papers smoothly placed. The pigeon holes were deep, and, removing the files of documents, I groped into their recesses. Presently I felt something there, and dragged it out. It was an old bandana handkerchief, heavy and knotted. I opened it, and saw it was a savings' bank.

I now recalled all the quiet mysteries which I had noted in the man. I remembered that he never spoke but to answer; that though at intervals he had considerable time to himself, yet I had never seen him reading – no, not even a newspaper; that for long periods he would stand looking out, at his pale window behind the screen, upon the dead brick wall; I was quite sure he never visited any refectory or eating-house; while his pale face clearly indicated that he never drank beer like Turkey, or tea and coffee even, like other men; that he never went anywhere in particular that I could learn; never went out for a walk, unless indeed that was the case at present; that he had declined telling who he was, or whence he came, or whether he had any relatives in the world; that though so thin and pale, he never complained of ill health. And more than all, I remembered a certain unconscious air of pallid – how shall I call it? – of pallid haughtiness, say, or rather an austere reserve about him, which had positively awed me into my tame compliance with his eccentricities, when I had feared to ask him to do the slightest incidental thing for me, even though I might know, from his long-continued motionlessness, that behind his screen he must be standing in one of those dead-wall reveries of his.

Revolving all these things, and coupling them with the recently discovered fact that he made my office his constant abiding place and home, and not forgetful of his morbid moodiness; revolving all these things, a prudential feeling began to steal over me. My first emotions had been those of pure melancholy and sincerest pity; but just in proportion as the forlornness of Bartleby grew and grew to my imagination, did that same melancholy merge into fear, that pity into repulsion. So true it is, and so terrible, too, that up to a certain point the thought or sight of misery enlists our best affections; but, in certain special cases, beyond that point it does not. They err who would assert that invariably this is owing to the inherent selfishness of the human heart. It rather proceeds from a certain hopelessness of remedying excessive and organic ill. To a sensitive being, pity is not seldom pain. And when at last it is perceived that such pity cannot lead to effectual succour, common sense bids the soul be rid of it. What I saw that morning persuaded me that the scrivener was the victim of innate and incurable disorder. I might give alms to his body; but his body did not pain him; it was his soul that suffered, and his soul I could not reach.

I did not accomplish the purpose of going to Trinity Church that morning. Somehow, the things I had seen disqualified me for the time from church-going. I walked homeward, thinking what I would do with Bartleby. Finally, I resolved upon this: – I would put certain calm questions to him the next morning, touching his history, &c., and if he declined to answer them openly and unreservedly (and I supposed he would prefer not), then to give him a twenty dollar bill over and above whatever I might owe him, and tell him his services were no longer required; but that if in any other way I could assist him, I would be happy to do so, especially if he desired to return to his native place, wherever that might be, I would willingly help to defray the expenses. Moreover, if, after reaching home, he found himself at any time in want of aid, a letter from him would be sure of a reply.

The next morning came.

"Bartleby," said I, gently calling to him behind his screen.

No reply.

"Bartleby," said I, in a still gentler tone, "come here; I am not going to ask you to do anything you would prefer not to do – I simply wish to speak to you."

Upon this he noiselessly slid into view.

"Will you tell me, Bartleby, where you were born?"

"I would prefer not to."

"Will you tell me *anything* about yourself?"

"I would prefer not to..'

"But what reasonable objection can you have to speak to me? I feel friendly towards you."

He did not look at me while I spoke, but kept his glance fixed upon my bust of Cicero, which, as I then sat, was directly behind me, some six inches above my head.

"What is your answer, Bartleby?" said I, after waiting a considerable time for a reply, during which his countenance remained immovable, only there was the faintest conceivable tremor of the white attenuated mouth.

·"At present I prefer to give no answer," he said, and retired into his hermitage.

It was rather weak in me I confess, but his manner on this occasion nettled me. Not only did there seem to lurk in it a certain calm disdain, but his perverseness seemed ungrateful, considering the undeniable good usage and indulgence he had received from me.

Again I sat ruminating what I should do. Mortified as I was at his behaviour, and resolved as I had been to dismiss him when I entered my office, nevertheless I strangely felt something superstitious knocking at my heart, and forbidding me to carry out my purpose, and denouncing me for a villain if I dared to breathe one bitter word against this forlornest of mankind. At last, familiarly drawing my chair behind his screen, I sat down and said: "Bartleby, never mind then about revealing your history; but let me entreat you, as a friend, to comply as far as may be with the usages of this office. Say now you will help to examine papers to-morrow

170

or next day: in short, say now that in a day or two you will begin to be a little reasonable: – say so, Bartleby."

"At present I would prefer not to be a little reasonable," was his mildly cadaverous reply.

... The next day I noticed that Bartleby did nothing but stand at his window in his dead-wall revery. Upon asking him why he did not write, he said that he had decided upon doing no more writing.

"Why, how now? what next?" exclaimed I, "do no more writing?"

"No more."

"And what is the reason?"

"Do you not see the reason for yourself?" he indifferently replied.

I looked steadfastly at him, and perceived that his eyes looked dull and glazed. Instantly it occurred to me, that his unexampled diligence in copying by his dim window for the first few weeks of his stay with me might have temporarily impaired his vision.

I was touched. I said something in condolence with him. I hinted that, of course, he did wisely in abstaining from writing for a while, and urged him to embrace that opportunity of taking wholesome exercise in the open air. This, however, he did not do. A few days after this, my other clerks being absent, and being in a great hurry to despatch certain letters by the mail, I thought that, having nothing else earthly to do, Bartleby would surely be less inflexible than usual, and carry these letters to the Post Office. But he blankly declined. So, much to my inconvienience, I went myself.

Still added days went by. Whether Bartleby's eyes improved or not, I could not say. To all appearance, I thought they did. But when I asked him if they did, he vouchsafed no answer. At all events, he would do no copying. At last, in reply to my urgings, he informed me that he had permanently given up copying.

"What!" exclaimed I; "suppose your eyes should get entirely well – better than ever before – would you not copy then?"

"I have given up copying," he answered and slid aside.

He remained, as ever, a fixture in my chamber. Nay – if that were possible – he became still more of a fixture than before. What was to be done? He would do nothing in the office: why should he stay there? In plain fact, he had now become a millstone to me, not only useless as a necklace, but afflictive to bear. Yet I was sorry for him. I speak less than truth when I say that, on his own account, he occasioned me uneasiness. If he would but have named a single relative or friend, I would instantly have written, and urged their taking the poor fellow away to some convenient retreat. But he seemed alone, absolutely alone in the universe. A bit of wreckage in the mid-Atlantic. At length, necessities connected with my business tyrannized over all other considerations. Decently as I could, I told Bartleby that in six days' time he must unconditionally leave the office. I warned him to take measures, in the interval, for procuring some other abode. I offered to assist him in this endeavour, if he himself would but take the first step towards a removal. "And when you finally quit me, Bartleby," added I, "I shall see that you go away not entirely unprovided. Six days from this hour, remember."

At the expiration of that period, I peeped behind the screen, and lo! Bartleby was there.

I buttoned up my coat, balanced myself; advanced slowly towards him, touched his shoulder, and said, "The time has come; you must quit this place; I am sorry for you; here is money; but you must go."

"I would prefer not," he replied, with his back still towards me.

"You *must*."

He remained silent.

Now I had an unbounded confidence in this man's common honesty. He had frequently restored to me sixpences and shillings carelessly dropped upon the floor, for I am apt to be very reckless in such shirt-button affairs. The proceeding then which followed will not be deemed extraordinary.

"Bartleby," said I, "I owe you twelve dollars on account; here are thirty-two; the odd twenty are yours. – Will you take it?" and I handed the bills towards him.

But he made no motion.

"I will leave them here then," putting them under a weight on the table. Then taking my hat and cane and going to the door, I tranquilly turned and added – "After you have removed your things from these offices, Bartleby, you will of course lock the door – since every one is now gone for the day but you – and if you please, slip your key underneath the mat, so that I may have it in the morning. I shall not see you again; so good-bye to you. If hereafter in your new place of abode I can be of any service to you, do not fail to advise me by letter. Good-bye, Bartleby, and fare you well."

But he answered not a word; like the last column of some ruined temple, he remained standing mute and solitary in the middle of the otherwise deserted room.

As I walked home in a pensive mood, my vanity got the better of my pity. I could not but highly plume myself on my masterly management in getting rid of Bartleby. Masterly I call it, and such it must appear to any dispassionate thinker. The beauty of my procedure seemed to consist in its perfect quietness. There was no vulgar bullying, no bravado of any sort, no choleric hectoring, no striding to and fro across the apartment, jerking out vehement commands for Bartleby to bundle himself off with his beggarly traps. Nothing of the kind. Without loudly bidding Bartleby depart – as an inferior genius might have done – I *assumed* the ground that depart he must; and upon that assumption built all I had to say. The more I thought over my procedure, the more I was charmed with it. Nevertheless, next morning, upon awakening, I had my doubts, – I had somehow slept off the fumes of vanity. One of the coolest and wisest hours a man has, is just after he awakes in the morning. My procedure seemed as sagacious as ever, – but only in theory. How it would prove in practice – there was the rub. It was truly a beautiful thought to have assumed Bartleby's departure; but, after all, that assumption was simply my own, and none of Bartleby's. The great point was, not whether I had assumed that he would quit me, but whether he would prefer so to do. He was more a man of preferences than assumptions.

After breakfast, I walked down town, arguing the probabilities *pro* and *con*. One moment I thought it would prove a miserable failure, and Bartleby would be found all alive at my office as usual; the next moment it seemed certain that I should see his chair empty. And so I kept veering about. At the corner of Broadway and Canal Street, I saw quite an excited group of people standing in earnest conversation.

"I'll take odds he doesn't," said a voice as I passed.

"Doesn't go? – done!" said I, "put up your money."

I was instinctively putting my hand in my pocket to produce my own, when I remembered that this was an election day. The words I had overheard bore no reference to Bartleby, but to the success or non-success of some candidate for the mayoralty. In my intent frame of mind, I had, as it were, imagined that all Broadway shared in my excitement, and were debating the same question with me. I passed on, very thankful that the uproar of the street screened my momentary absent-mindedness.

As I had intended, I was earlier than usual at my office door. I stood listening for a moment. All was still. He must be gone. I tried the knob. The door was locked. Yes, my procedure had worked to a charm; he indeed must be vanished. Yet a certain

173

melancholy mixed with this: I was almost sorry for my brilliant success. I was fumbling under the door mat for the key, which Bartleby was to have left there for me, when accidentally my knee knocked against a panel, producing a summoning sound, and in response a voice came to me from within – "Not yet; I am occupied."

It was Bartleby.

I was thunderstruck. For an instant I stood like the man who, pipe in mouth, was killed one cloudless afternoon long ago in Virginia, by summer lightning; at his own warm open window he was killed, and remained leaning out there upon the dreamy afternoon, till some one touched him, and he fell.

"Not gone!" I murmured at last. But again obeying that wondrous ascendency which the inscrutable scrivener had over me – and from which ascendency, for all my chafing, I could not completely escape – I slowly went down stairs and out into the street, and while walking round the block, considered what I should next do in this unheard-of perplexity. Turn the man out by an actual thrusting I could not; to drive him away by calling him hard names would not do; calling in the police was an unpleasant idea; and yet permit him to enjoy his cadaverous triumph over me, – this too I could not think of. What was to be done? or, if nothing could be done, was there anything further that I could *assume* in the matter? Yes, as before I had prospectively assumed that Bartleby would depart, so now I might retrospectively assume that departed he was. In the legitimate carrying out of this assumption, I might enter my office in a great hurry, and pretending not to see Bartleby at all, walk straight against him as if he were air. Such a proceeding would in a singular degree have the appearance of a home-thrust. It was hardly possible that Bartleby could withstand such an application of the doctrine of assumptions. But, upon second thought, the success of the plan seemed rather dubious. I resolved to argue the matter over with him again.

"Bartleby," said I, entering the office, with a quietly severe expression, "I am seriously displeased. I am pained, Bartleby. I had thought better of you. I had imagined you of such a gentlemanly organization, that in any delicate dilemma a slight hint would suffice – in short, an assumption; but it appears I am deceived. Why," I added, unaffectedly starting, "you have not even touched that money yet," pointing to it, just where I had left it the evening previous.

He answered nothing.

176

"Will you, or will you not, quit me?" I now demanded in a sudden passion, advancing close to him.

"I would prefer *not* to quit you," he replied, gently emphasizing the *not*.

"What earthly right have you to stay here? Do you pay any rent? Do you pay my taxes? Or is this property yours?"

He answered nothing.

"Are you ready to go on and write now? Are your eyes recovered? Could you copy a small paper for me this morning? or help examine a few lines? or step round to the Post Office? In a word, will you do anything at all, to give a colouring to your refusal to depart the premises?"

He silently retired into his hermitage.

I was now in such a state of nervous resentment that I thought it but prudent to check myself, at present, from further demonstrations. Bartleby and I were alone. I remembered the tragedy of the unfortunate Adams and the still more unfortunate Colt in the solitary office of the latter; and how poor Colt, being dreadfully incensed by Adams, and imprudently permitting himself to get wildly excited, was at unawares hurried into his fatal act – an act which certainly no man could possibly deplore more than the actor himself. Often it had occurred to me in my ponderings upon the subject, that had that altercation taken place in the public street, or at a private residence, it would not have terminated as it did. It was the circumstance of being alone in a solitary office, upstairs of a building entirely unhallowed by humanizing domestic associations – an uncarpeted office, doubtless, of a dusty, haggard sort of appearance; – this it must have been, which greatly helped to enhance the irritable desperation of the hapless Colt...

... Some days now passed, during which at leisure intervals I looked a little into "Edwards on the Will," and "Priestley on Necessity." Under the circumstances, those books induced a salutary feeling. Gradually I slid into the persuasion that these troubles of mine, touching the scrivener, had been all predestinated from eternity, and Bartleby was billeted upon me for some mysterious purpose of an all-wise Providence, which it was not for a mere mortal like me to fathom. Yes, Bartleby, stay there behind your screen, thought I; I shall persecute you no more; you are harmless and noiseless as any of these old chairs; in short, I never feel so private as when I know you are here. At least I see it, I feel it; I penetrate to the predestinated purpose of my life. I am content. Others may have loftier parts to enact; but my mission in this world, Bartleby, is to furnish you with office room for such period as you may see fit to remain.

I believe that this wise and blessed frame of mind would have continued with me had it not been for the unsolicited and uncharitable remarks obtruded upon me by my professional friends who visited the rooms. But thus it often is, that the constant friction of illiberal minds wears out at last the best resolves of the more generous. Though to be sure, when I reflected upon it, it was not strange that people entering my office should be struck by the peculiar aspect of the unaccountable Bartleby, and so be tempted to throw out some sinister observations concerning him. Sometimes an attorney having business with me, and calling at my office, and finding no one but the scrivener there, would undertake to obtain some sort of precise information from him touching my whereabouts; but without heeding his idle talk, Bartleby would remain standing immovable in the middle of the room. So, after contemplating him in that position for a time, the attorney would depart, no wiser than he came.

Also, when a Reference was going on, and the room full of lawyers and witnesses and business was driving fast, some deeply occupied legal gentleman present, seeing Bartleby wholly unemployed, would request him to run round to his (the legal gentleman's) office and fetch some papers for him. Thereupon, Bartleby would tranquilly decline, and yet remain idle as before. Then the lawyer would give a great stare, and turn to me. And what could I say? At last I was made aware that all through the circle of my professional acquaintance, a whisper of wonder was running round, having reference to the strange creature I kept at my office. This worried me very much. And as the idea came upon me of his possibly turning out a long-lived man, and keep occupying my chambers, and denying my authority; and perplexing my visitors; and scandalizing my professional reputation; and casting a general gloom over the premises; keeping soul and body together to the last upon his savings (for doubtless he spent but half a dime a day), and in the end perhaps outlive me, and claim posesssion of my office by right of his perpetual occupancy: as all these dark anticipations crowded upon me more and more, and my friends continually intruded their relentless remarks upon the apparition in my room, a great change was wrought in me. I resolved to gather all my faculties together, and for ever rid me of this intolerable incubus.

Ere revolving any complicated project, however, adapted to this end, I first simply suggested to Bartleby the propriety of his permanent departure. In a calm and serious tone, I commended the idea to his careful and mature consideration. But having taken three days to meditate upon it, he apprised me that his original determination remained the same; in short, that he still preferred to abide with me.

What shall I do? I now said to myself, buttoning up my coat to the last button. What shall I do? what ought I to do? what does conscience say I *should* do with this man, or rather ghost? Rid myself of him, I must; go, he shall. But how? You will not thrust him, the poor, pale, passive mortal, – you will not thrust such a helpless creature out of your door? you will not dishonour yourself by such cruelty? No, I will not, I cannot do that. Rather would I let him live and die here, and then mason up his remains in the wall. What then will you do? For all your coaxing, he will not budge. Bribes he leaves under your own paper-weight on your table; in short, it is quite plain that he prefers to cling to you.

Then something severe, something unusual must be done. What! surely you will not have him collared by a constable, and commit his innocent pallor to the common jail? And upon what ground could you procure such a thing to be done? – a vagrant, is he? What! he a vagrant, a wanderer, who refuses to budge? It is because he will *not* be a vagrant, then, that you seek to count him *as* a vagrant. That is too absurd. No visible means of support: there I have him. Wrong again: for indubitably he *does* support himself, and that is the only unanswerable proof that any man can show of his possessing the means so to do. No more then. Since he will not quit me, I must quit him. I will change my offices; I will move elsewhere; and give him fair notice, that if I find him on my new premises I will then proceed against him as a common trespasser.

Acting accordingly, next day I thus addressed him: "I find these chambers too far from the City Hall; the air is unwholesome. In a word, I propose to remove my offices next week, and shall no longer require your services. I tell you this now, in order that you may seek another place."

He made no reply, and nothing more was said.

On the appointed day I engaged carts and men, proceeded to my chambers, and having but little furniture, everything was removed in a few hours. Throughout all, the scrivener remained standing behind the screen, which I directed to be removed the last thing. It was withdrawn; and being folded up like a huge folio, left him the motionless occupant of a naked room. I stood in the entry

179

watching him a moment, while something from within me up-braided me.

I re-entered, with my hand in my pocket – and – and my heart in my mouth.

"Good-bye, Bartleby; I am going – good-bye, and God some way bless you; and take that," slipping something in his hand. But it dropped upon the floor and then – strange to say – I tore myself from him whom I had so longed to be rid of.

Established in my new quarters, for a day or two I kept the door locked, and started at every footfall in the passages. When I returned to my rooms after any little absence, I would pause at the threshold for an instant, and attentively listen, ere applying my key. But these fears were needless. Bartleby never came nigh me.

I thought all was going well, when a perturbed looking stranger visited me, inquiring whether I was the person who had recently occupied rooms at No. – Wall street.

Full of forebodings, I replied that I was.

"Then sir," said the stranger, who proved a lawyer, "you are responsible for the man you left there. He refuses to do any copying, he refuses to do anything; and he says he prefers not to; and he refuses to quit the premises."

"I am very sorry, sir," said I, with assumed tranquillity, but an inward tremor, "but, really, the man you allude to is nothing to me – he is no relation or apprentice of mine, that you should hold me responsible for him."

"In mercy's name, who is he?"

"I certainly cannot inform you. I know nothing about him. Formerly I employed him as a copyist; but he has done nothing for me now for some time past."

"I shall settle him then, – good morning, sir."

Several days passed, and I heard nothing more; and though I often felt a charitable prompting to call at the place and see poor Bartleby, yet a certain squeamishness of I know not what withheld me.

All is over with him, by this time, thought I at last, when through another week no further intelligence reached me. But coming to my room the day after, I found several persons waiting at my door in a high state of nervous excitement.

"That's the man – here he comes," cried the foremost one, whom I recognized as the lawyer who had previously called upon me alone.

"You must take him away, sir, at once," cried a portly person among them, advancing upon me, and whom I knew to be the

180

landlord of No. – Wall street. "These gentlemen, my tenants, cannot stand it any longer; Mr. B –," pointing to the lawyer, "has turned him out of his room, and he now persists in haunting the building generally, sitting upon the banisters of the stairs by day, and sleeping in the entry by night. Everybody here is concerned; clients are leaving the offices; some fears are entertained of a mob; something you must do, and that without delay."

Aghast at this torrent, I fell back before it, and would fain have locked myself in my new quarters. In vain I persisted that Bartleby was nothing to me – no more than to any one else there. In vain: – I was the last person known to have anything to do with him, and they held me to the terrible account. Fearful then of being exposed in the papers (as one person present obscurely threatened) I considered the matter, and at length said, that if the lawyer would give me a confidential interview with the scrivener, in his (the lawyer's) own room, I would that afternoon strive my best to rid them of the nuisance they complained of.

Going upstairs to my old haunt, there was Bartleby silently sitting upon the banister at the landing.

"What are you doing here, Bartleby?" said I.

"Sitting upon the banister," he mildly replied.

I motioned him into the lawyer's room, who then left us.

"Bartleby," said I, "are you aware that you are the cause of great tribulation to me, by persisting in occupying the entry after being dismissed from the office?"

No answer.

"Now one of two things must take place. Either you must do something, or something must be done to you. Now what sort of business would you like to engage in? Would you like to re-engage in copying for some one?"

"No; I would prefer not to make any change."

"Would you like a clerkship in a dry-goods store?"

"There is too much confinement about that. No, I would not like a clerkship; but I am not particular."

"Too much confinement," I cried, "why you keep yourself confined all the time!"

"I would prefer not to take a clerkship," he rejoined, as if to settle that little item at once.

"How would a bartender's business suit you? There is no trying of the eyesight in that."

"I would not like it at all; though, as I said before, I am not particular."

181

His unwonted wordiness inspirited me. I returned to the charge.

"Well then, would you like to travel through the country collecting bills for the merchants? That would improve your health."

"No, I would prefer to be doing something else."

"How then would going as a companion to Europe to entertain some young gentleman with your conversation, – how would that suit you?"

"Not at all. It does not strike me that there is anything definite about that. I like to be stationary. But I am not particular."

"Stationary you shall be then," I cried, now losing all patience, and for the first time in all my exasperating connection with him fairly flying into a passion. "If you do not go away from these premises before night, I shall feel bound – indeed I *am* bound – to – to – to quit the premises myself!" I rather absurdly concluded, knowing not with what possible threat to try to frighten his immobility into compliance. Despairing of all further efforts, I was precipitately leaving him, when a final thought occurred to me – one which had not been wholly unindulged before.

"Bartleby," said I, in the kindest tone I could assume under such exciting circumstances, "will you go home with me now – not to my office, but my dwelling – and remain there till we can conclude upon some convenient arrangement for you at our leisure? Come, let us start now, right away."

"No: at present I would prefer not to make any change at all."

I answered nothing; but effectually dodging every one by the suddenness and rapidity of my flight, rushed from the building, ran up Wall street toward Broadway, and then jumping into the first omnibus was soon removed from pursuit. As soon as tranquillity returned I distinctly perceived that I had now done all that I possibly could, both in respect to the demands of the landlord and his tenants, and with regard to my own desire and sense of duty, to benefit Bartleby, and shield him from rude persecution. I now strove to be entirely care-free and quiescent; and my conscience justified me in the attempt; though indeed it was not so successful as I could have wished. So fearful was I of being again hunted out by the incensed landlord and his exasperated tenants, that, surrendering my business to Nippers, for a few days I drove about the upper part of the town and through the suburbs, in my rockaway; crossed over to Jersey City and Hoboken, and paid fugitive visits to Manhattanville and Astoria. In fact I almost lived in my rockaway for the time.

When again I entered my office, lo, a note from the landlord lay upon the desk. I opened it with trembling hands. It informed me that the writer had sent to the police, and had Bartleby removed to the Tombs as a vagrant. Moreover, since I knew more about him than anyone else, he wished me to appear at that place, and make a suitable statement of the facts. These tidings had a conflicting effect upon me. At first I was indignant; but at last almost approved. The landlord's energetic, summary dispostition had led him to adopt a procedure which I do not think I would have decided upon myself; and yet as a last resort, under such peculiar circumstances, it seemed the only plan.

As I afterwards learned, the poor scrivener, when told that he must be conducted to the Tombs, offered not the slightest obstacle, but in his own pale, unmoving way silently acquiesced.

Some of the compassionate and curious bystanders joined the party; and headed by one of the constables, arm-in-arm with Bartleby the silent procession filed its way through all the noise, and heat, and joy of the roaring thoroughfares at noon.

The same day I received the note I went to the Tombs, or, to speak more properly, the Halls of Justice. Seeking the right officer, I stated the purpose of my call, and was informed that the individual I described was indeed within. I then assured the functionary that Bartleby was a perfectly honest man, and greatly to be a compassionated (however unaccountable) eccentric. I narrated all I knew, and closed by suggesting the idea of letting him remain in as indulgent confinement as possible till something less harsh might be done – though indeed I hardly knew what. At all events if nothing else could be decided upon, the alms-house must receive him. I then begged to have an interview.

Being under no disgraceful charge, and quite serene and harmless in all his ways, they had permitted him freely to wander about the prison, and especially in the enclosed grass-platted yards thereof. And so I found him there, standing all alone in the quietest of the yards, his face toward a high wall – while all around, from the narrow slits of the jail windows, I thought I saw peering out upon him the eyes of murderers and thieves.

"Bartleby!"

"I know you," he said, without looking round, – "and I want nothing to say to you."

"It was not I that brought you here, Bartleby," said I, keenly pained at his implied suspicion. "And to you, this should not be so vile a place. Nothing reproachful attaches to you by being here.

And see, it is not so sad a place as one might think. Look, there is the sky and here is the grass."

"I know where I am," he replied, but would say nothing more, and so I left him.

As I entered the corridor again a broad, meat-like man in an apron accosted me, and jerking his thumb over his shoulder said – "Is that your friend?"

"Yes."

"Does he want to starve? If he does, let him live on the prison fare, that's all."

"Who are you?" asked I, not knowing what to make of such an unofficially speaking person in such a place.

"I am the grub-man. Such gentlemen as have friends here, hire me to provide them with something good to eat."

"Is this so?" said I, turning to the turnkey.

He said it was.

"Well then," said I, slipping some silver into the grubman's hands (for so they called him), "I want you to give particular attention to my friend there; let him have the best dinner you can get. And you must be as polite to him as possible."

"Introduce me, will you?" said the grub-man, looking at me with an expression which seemed to say he was all impatience for an opportunity to give a specimen of his breeding.

Thinking it would prove of benefit to the scrivener, I acquiesced; and asking the grub-man his name, went up with him to Bartleby.

"Bartleby, this is Mr. Cutlets; you will find him very useful to you."

"Your sarvant, sir, your sarvant," said the grub-man, making a low salutation behind his apron. "Hope you find it pleasant here, sir; – spacious grounds – cool apartments, sir – hope you'll stay with us some time – try to make it agreeable. May Mrs. Cutlets and I have the pleasure of your company to dinner, sir, in Mrs. Cutlets' private room?"

"I prefer not to dine to-day," said Bartleby, turning away. "It would disagree with me; I am unused to dinners." So saying, he slowly moved to the other side of the enclosure and took up a position fronting the dead-wall.

"How's this?" said the grub-man, addressing me with a stare of astonishment. "He's odd, ain't he?"

"I think he is a little deranged," said I, sadly.

"Deranged? deranged is it? Well now, upon my word, I thought that friend of yourn was a gentleman forger; they are always pale and genteel-like, them forgers. I can't help pity 'em – can't help it, sir. Did you know Monroe Edwards?" he added touchingly, and paused. Then, laying his hand pityingly on my shoulder, sighed, "he died of the consumption at Sing-Sing. So you weren't acquainted with Monroe?"

"No, I was never socially acquainted with any forgers. But I cannot stop longer. Look to my friend yonder. You will not lose by it. I will see you again."

Some few days after this, I again obtained admission to the Tombs, and went through the corridors in quest of Bartleby; but without finding him.

"I saw him coming from his cell not long ago." said a turnkey, "maybe he's gone to loiter in the yards."

So I went in that direction.

"Are you looking for the silent man?" said another turnkey passing me. "Yonder he lies – sleeping in the yard there. 'Tis not twenty minutes since I saw him lie down."

The yard was entirely quiet. It was not accessible to the common prisoners. The surrounding walls, of amazing thickness, kept off all sounds behind them. The Egyptian character of the masonry weighed upon me with its gloom. But a soft imprisoned turf grew under foot. The heart of the eternal pyramids, it seemed, wherein by some strange magic, through the clefts grass-seed, dropped by birds, had sprung.

Strangely huddled at the base of the wall – his knees drawn up, and lying on his side, his head touching the cold stones – I saw the wasted Bartleby. But nothing stirred. I paused; then went close up to him; stooped over, and saw that his dim eyes were open; otherwise he seemed profoundly sleeping. Something prompted me to touch him. I felt his hand when a tingling shiver ran up my arm and down my spine to my feet.

The round face of the grub-man peered upon me now. "His dinner is ready. Won't he dine to-day, either? Or does he live without dining?"

"Lives without dining," said I, and closed the eyes.

"Eh! – He's asleep, ain't he?"

"With kings and counsellors." murmured I...

...I hardly know whether I should divulge one little item of rumour, which came to my ear a few months after the scrivener's decease. Upon what basis it rested, I could never ascertain; and hence, how true it is I cannot now tell. But inasmuch as this vague report has not been without a certain strange suggestive interest to me, however sad, it may prove the same with some others; and so I will briefly mention it. The report was this: that Bartleby had been a subordinate clerk in the Dead Letter Office at Washington, from which he had been suddenly removed by a change in the administration. When I think over this rumour I cannot adequately express the emotions which seize me. Dead letters! does it not sound like dead men? Conceive a man by nature and misfortune prone to a pallid hopelessness: can any business seem more fitted to heighten it than that of continually handling these dead letters, and assorting them for the flames? For by the cartload they are annually burned. Sometimes from out the folded paper the pale clerk takes a ring: – the finger it was meant for, perhaps, moulders in the grave; a bank-note sent in swiftest charity: – he whom it would relieve, nor eats nor hungers any more; pardon for those who died despairing; hope for those who died unhoping; good tidings for those who died stifled by unrelieved calamities. On errands of life, these letters speed to death.

Ah Bartleby! Ah humanity!

Thine
do these inexplicable fleshly bonds

Vh.Mr.

~.

N. B. I aint crazy.

Bibliography

American

Works by Herman Melville

Billy Budd (in *Four Great American Novels*). Raymond W. Short, ed., New York, Henry Holt & Co., 1946.

Collected Poems. Howard P. Vincent, ed., New York, Hendricks House, Inc., 1946.

The Confidence-Man: His Masquerade. New York, Grove Press, Inc., 1949.

Encantadas. Palo Alto, Calif., Wiliam P. Wreden.

Israel Potter: His Fifty Years of Exile. New York, Farrar, Straus & Cudahy, Inc., (L. C. Page), 1905.

Journal of a Visit to Europe and the Levant. H. Horsford, ed., Princeton, N.J., Princeton University Press, 1954.

Mardi. New York, Farrar, Straus & Cuhady, Inc., (L. C. Page) 1923.

Moby Dick; or, the White Whale. New York, Farrar, Straus & Cudahy, Inc., (L. C. Page), 1900.

Moby Dick. New York, Random House, Inc., (Modern Library), 1930.

Omoo: A Narrative of Adventures in the South Seas. New York, Farrar, Straus & Cudahy, Inc., (L. C. Page), 1900.

Omoo. New York, Grove Press, Inc., 1958.

Piazza Tales. Egbert S. Oliver, ed., New York, Hendricks House, Inc., 1948.

Pierre; or, The Ambiguities. New York, Grove Press, Inc., 1957.

Portable Melville. (*Typee, Billy Budd,* poems, stories, letters, journals & other writings) Jay Leyda, ed., New York, Viking Press, Inc., 1952.

Redburn, his First Voyage. New York, Farrar, Straus & Cudahy, Inc., (L. C. Page) 1924.

Selected Writings. New York, Random House, Inc., (Modern Library), 1952.

Typee. New York, E. P. Dutton & Co., Inc., (Everyman's Library).

Typee: A Real Romance of the South Sea. New York, Farrar, Straus & Cudahy, Inc., (L. C. Page) 1900.

White Jacket; or, The World in a Man-of-War. New York, Farrar, Straus & Cudahy, Inc., (L. C. Page) 1900.

White Jacket; or, The World in a Man-of-War. New York, Grove Press, Inc., 1952.

Selected Studies of Herman Melville

Arvin, Newton. *Herman Melville.* New York, William Sloane Associates, 1950.

Chase, Richard. *Herman Melville: A Critical Study.* New York, Macmillan Co.

Howard, Leon. *Herman Melville: A Biography.* Los Angeles, University of California Press.

Leyda, Jay, ed. *The Melville Log: A Documentary Life of Herman Melville.* 2 Vols. Harcourt Brace, New York, 1951.

Metcalf, E. M. *Herman Melville: Cycle and Epicycle.* Cambridge, Mass., Harvard University Press, 1953.

Olson, Charles. *Call Me Ishmael.* New York, Grove Press, Inc., 1958.

Weaver, Raymond. *Herman Melville: Mariner and Mystic.* New York, 1921 (op).

British

Works by Herman Melville

Billy Budd & Other Stories. John Lehmann, 1951.

Billy Budd, Foretopman. John Lehmann, 1946.

The Complete Stories of Herman Melville. Eyre & Spottiswoode, 1951.

The Confidence-Man: His Masquerade. London, Evergreen Books; John Calder, 1958.

Journal of a Visit to London and the Continent, 1849–50. (ed. Eleanor Melville Metcalf) Cohen & West, 1949.

Library Edition of Herman Melville's works. Cape, 1924.

Moby Dick. Collins, 1953.

Moby Dick. Dent, (Everyman's Library) 1954.

Omoo. London, Evergreen Books; John Calder, 1958.

Pierre; or the Ambiguities. London, Evergreen Books; John Calder, 1958.

Selected Poems of Herman Melville. (ed. William Plomer). Hogarth Press, 1943.

Typee. Dent, (Everyman's Library) 1949.

White Jacket; or the World in a Man-of-War. London, Evergreen Books; John Calder, 1958.

Selected Studies of Herman Melville

Arvin, Newton. *Herman Melville.* Methuen, 1950.

Brooks, Van Wyck. *The Times of Melville and Whitman.* Dent, 1948.

Levin, Harry T. *The Power of Blackness: Hawthorne, Poe, Melville.* Faber, 1958.

Mason, Ronald C. *The Spirit above the Dust: a study of Herman Melville.* John Lehmann, 1951.

Olson, Charles. *Call Me Ishmael.* London, Evergreen Books; John Calder, 1958.

A Note on Illustrations

We wish to thank the following authors, editors and organisations, for permission to reproduce the many illustrations in this volume:

Jay Leyda, *The Melville Log* (Harcourt Brace, New York, 1951), pp. 6, 13, 59, 62, 121, 122, 186.

John A. Kouwenhoven, *The Columbia Historical Portrait of New York* (Doubleday, New York, 1953), pp. 19, 157, 161, 166.

Robert Marin, ed., H. Melville, *Mardi*, with jacket design by Max Ernst p. 130.

Brooks, *Our Literary Heritage* (Dutton, New York), pp. 22, 46, 47, 52, 70, 85, 127.

Editions de Paris: pp. 3 of the inside cover, 73, 76-7, 88-9, 90, 96, 131, 149.

Berkshire Atheneum, Pittsfield, Mass.: pp. 12, 13, 15, 27, 67, 95, 150.

Old Dartmouth Historical Society, New-Bedford, Mass.: pp. 9, 58, 79, 80, 94, 146.

Library of Harvard University: pp. 124, 129.

Collections of the Library of Congress: pp. 10, 116, 174-5.

British Council: pp. 24, 125.

Bibliothèque Nationale: pp. 2 of inside cover, 17, 28-9, 31, 34, 36, 38-9, 41, 53, 56, 57, 101, 104, 115, 154-5.

Cahiers du Cinéma: 139, 147.

Alinari-Giraudon: p. 120.

Tate Gallery: pp. 97, 107, 110.

Boosey & Hawkes: p. 127.

On page 2 is reproduced a letter from Melville to his daughter, Bessie.